As Luck Would Have It

A catalogue record of this book is available from the British Library

First Edition: September 2003

ISBN: 1-84375-054-6

To order additional copies of this book please visit:
http://www.upso.co.uk/bobluck

Published by: UPSO Ltd
5 Stirling Road, Castleham Business Park,
St Leonards-on-Sea, East Sussex TN38 9NW - UK
Tel: 01424 853349 Fax: 0870 191 3991
Email: info@upso.co.uk Web: http://www.upso.co.uk

XMAS 2003

To

JIM + JOYCE

WITH LOTS OF LOVE

FROM

Aunt Doris XXX

Evelyn Luck

As Luck Would Have It

Written by Colin Roberts

UPSO

Contents

For Julie in memory of her father

Foreword

When I was first asked to write this biography I knew only that Bob Luck was a cider maker, a Kentish man who everyone, seemed to have heard of. I knew of him like many people of this region did, through his cider alone. There was something very special about the mellow potent liqueur cider that was unmatched anywhere in the country; but the man was special too.

What I had not appreciated was that there were two men, two Bob Luck's, father and son, and I was to write about the son. My first dilemma was to try to separate the activities of the two, for both were jokers, the son, young Bob being a microcosm of the father, old Bob. The conclusion I reached over the ensuing weeks was that truly 'Man *is* immortal through his sons.' Indeed I gained the impression old Bob did not always like what he saw in his eldest son, simply because the learned behaviour of the younger Bob was a mirror of himself.

This then is the biography of 'young Bob Luck' as told to me by his widow Evelyn and others. Of course no one could know Bob without being sucked into his life in one way or another, so a good deal of this work deals with the product of that vacuum.

A word about country humour: Having had a foot in both camps, so to speak, Town and country. It has become more apparent to me that humour comes in different guises; subtle, sophisticated, accidental, deliberate, dangerous, rude coarse and so on. Whereas town humour is nearly always a related humour, country humour is nearly always visual. If I dared to categorise country humour it would be to say it equates to circus humour without the audience.

Introduction

We none of us can choose the year into which we are born and even if parents were astrological in their thinking even they, in the case of the newly born Robert Luck could not have predicted the discovery of the new planet 'Pluto' that same year.

Nineteen thirty was as busy a year as any other. Arsenal won the FA cup, winning two goals to nil against Huddersfield Town.

Jack Hobbs scored his 54,921st run to beat WG Grace's record. England lost the Ashes. America won the America's Cup and the year old Labour government struggled with a dole queue of two million. The dole was 15/- a week and petrol was four pence ha-penny a gallon.

Labour and the Liberals were still arguing about electoral reform and Hitler's new copy of Mein Kamph was on sale at six old pence a copy, with, surprisingly, the royalties going to the Red Cross.

Happily none of these historical byelines was to trouble Mrs Freda [Dodo] Luck. These were the days when the predicted arrival of a new baby consisted of simple arithmetic from an obscure conception date, days without MRI and Ultra Sound checks on the baby's health and few qualified midwives.

August nineteen thirty had been one of the hottest on record in England. London reached the nineties. But it was a good month the new child might later argue to be born in the company of the big names to be, Neil Armstrong first man on the moon; Ted Hughes Poet laureate and Actor Sir Sean Connery.

Robert [Bob] Luck arrived in the early hours of the 17th August 1930 at Acton Farm Wittersham. Named after his father he was always destined to be referred to as 'young' Bob.

The Lucks were all farmers. Young Bob's grandfather farmed High Lees near Beltring Paddock Wood and his father who married Freda Brann farmed at Poplar Farm Wittersham which adjoined Acton the Brann's family home. The Brann's also owned Owley and built the Smitings. When grandfather Robert William died in 1922 his widow Flo moved with sons Bob,*[old Bob]* Sid and daughter Vera to Poplar Farm Wittersham from Bishopsden Benenden she and her then late husband having owned that and Frogs Hole Farm.

It is not difficult to see how the shared march's at Wittersham and the common farming interests of these two families became the focus for the great Luck cider making generation which started at Frogs Hole in 1935.

It was on July 24th this same year in a period of minor marital discord that young Bob's brother Michael was born at the Woolpack Public House Tenterden in the more serene surroundings of Freda Brann's own family who were the owners until 1945.

Young Bob Luck; making the feathers fly as usual

School Days – Benenden 1935-1944

Bob's first memories are of living at Frogs Hole Farm Benenden from where he attended Benenden primary school situated just off the village green. This was quite a walk for a young boy but common enough in the late thirties. Often he got a lift with other children on the lorry that went that way daily, starting out from Rolling's Stores [*now the post office stores*] in the village and doing the rounds with bread packed in a large tea chest with other general groceries mainly for Benenden hospital then a sanatorium.

The lorry which called in at Frogs Hole lane and other houses and lanes in the area had a canvas tilt and two rows of seats either side. This was thought to be an arrangement with the local parents to pick up children for school in Benenden. The driver was Nelson Mannering who like the school bus drivers of to-day had his work cut out controlling the children's natural exuberance. There was also room for two up front in the cab beside the driver a position that would be coveted by any young lad. However any that made the journey that way with Nelson was not there out of good behaviour but because he needed to be where he could be strictly observed.

Young Bob was one such lad and was quick to realise the advantages of being disruptive. In a child-like way he often turned such things to his advantage but not before incurring the wrath of the driver. Nelson Mannering was heard to shout on more then one occasion 'If you don't behave young Luck. I'll lugger you, yuh little bugger!' and often he did just that, Bob getting his ears boxed for his indiscipline.

In the years leading up to and during World War II, rabbits were always plentiful, myxomatosis didn't exist and indeed many large estates still employed warreners and would regard the taking of rabbits as poaching. Nevertheless country people regarded them as fair game and a good source of food.

Many young lads had ferrets, and young Bob was no exception. On some occasions he and his younger mate Jim Goodsell would skip off school and go rabbiting.

Bob would stuff the rabbit nets under his school jersey and the polecat Jill in his pocket, and then he and Jim would wait until the school transport in the form of Rolling's lorry had disappeared, knowing old Nelson Mannering wouldn't wait long for them. Then it was off into the woods to net a few bunnies which were later sold to local households with any left-overs going to the Benenden butcher Bill Reynolds for half a crown, [*12.5 new pence*] a kings ransom to lads of seven or eight in those days.

Of course they were clever enough not to turn up at home too early and as to their dishevelled appearance, well, this would be normal after a day at school and certainly would not have aroused suspicions.

Hardly a day went by without Bob getting into mischief and on one occasion he went off to the school with a pocket full of his dad's small bore cartridges. It was winter and he had a mind to play a trick on the teacher.

School classrooms in those days were heated often by cast iron pot-bellied stoves or in the case of Benenden primary a coke burner known as a turtle stove with a chimney leading out through the wall or ceiling with a cast iron top-plate to feed in the fuel.

On this particular morning Bob kept look out for the teacher and on seeing him approach quickly slid over the top-plate and threw in some of the cartridges. By the time Bob had returned to his desk the teacher had entered the classroom, only a few second elapsed before there was an almighty explosion which lifted the lid and blew out sparks, hot ash and coke around the classroom.

Young Bob's father played cricket for Benenden and would, like most cricketing fathers, have liked his son to follow him into the game. This was not to be, as old Bob's enthusiasm for fast bowling at his two sons standing one at a time with a bat in front of an old bushel apple box as a wicket wasn't thought by them to be very exciting; indeed the box was smashed to pieces more than once and soon young Bob decided this wasn't much fun and lost interest in the game. This did not however stop his mother sending him off with his father to the cricket matches and on one occasion at Benenden he and his school pal Brian Moore *[later to become the well known TV football commentator]* played together at the edge of the cricket field. The play became a 'rough and tumble' and later developed into a more serious fight which raged continuously around the cricket boundaries, much to the consternation of the spectators as these two incorrigible eight year olds threw punches at one another. Both ended up with bloody noses, more so young Bob as his was given to bleeding at the slightest knock. This incident turned out to be very embarrassing for his father and he was told to keep his unruly child in check which without doubt manifested itself in another lugging for Bob.

Bob tried hard at school but like many boys it didn't take much to distract him from the lesson in hand, more so if it was a subject that didn't interest him. One day he completely ruined the work-piece in the wood work class and the teacher was annoyed enough to give him a whack with the spoiled wood.

Bob was not slow to seize an opportunity when it suited him and to this end his fragile nose came in handy. On more than one occasion he had been given a cold flannel to hold on the back of his neck and made to lay out on the hammock outside the classroom until his bleeding nose abated, and was even given cold lemonade made by the sympathetic teacher's wife.

When the next woodwork lesson was due he came in for quite a bit of ribbing from his class mates, having incurred the wrath of the teacher last time for spoiling the work piece. *'You'd better make a better fist of it this time.' they jibed 'or you'll get another clout.'*

'Oh! Not likely! I'll get out of this one you'll see.' he said touching the side of his nose confidently.

On entering the class Bob gave his nose a tap and as

expected the blood was soon dripping freely onto the classroom floor. Of course as predicted he was given the first aid he knew he would receive and was soon laid back in the hammock sipping lemonade for all his class mates in the woodwork class to see through the windows. Bob had such control over his nose bleeds he never did woodwork again.

Frogs Hole had an air raid shelter, a relic from the war situated apart from the farm; they were still commonplace in gardens through out the country. Many of these Anderson shelters were by now converted into potting sheds, pig sties, chicken huts and so forth, but this one was the deserted HQ of boyhood adventurers. Bob and his brother Michael played a game where either their palls the Gosden brothers were the invaders or they the Luck brothers were. The idea was for the defenders to occupy the shelter against all odds. The odds however were German hand grenades, not real ones, in the form of clods of clay, thrown just as all boys throw stones at one another. The game had a habit of escalating and this day the Gosden brothers couldn't be shifted from their air raid shelter strong hold; not that is until young Bob went into the workshop and came out with a pan of brimstone which he set alight and pushed into the entrance of the shelter. Oh yes the enemy was defeated that time alright, coughing and spluttering out came the defeated Gosden brothers, probably shouting surrender or claiming foul.

Of course schooldays means schoolboy tricks and although the bucket over door trick was the stuff of Beano comics it was reserved for those papers; in them the target was nearly always the teacher.

Not so at Frogs Hole where they lived. Old Bob was always quite strict with the two brothers and they sought some sort of childhood revenge on their dad by setting the back door slightly ajar with the traditional bucket perched on top of the door leaning slightly against the wall and brimming with water. This delicate balance required there to be one of them each side of the door and it was young Bob on the inside as they set up the trap. As fate would have it their dad returned before they were ready and Michael young Bob's brother bolted for it, leaving young Bob stranded in the kitchen as old Bob entered. Down came the bucket to drench old Bob, the bucket bouncing off his shoulder and onto the now wet floor. Remember, buckets were two gallon and galvanised in those days.

Of course old Bob was livid and as young Bob dived for the door his way out was barred by his father who made sure his heavy size ten farm boot connected with his vagrant son's back side enough to launch him into the yard beyond.

Often in times of trouble young Bob sought refuge in the old orchard which bordered the wood at the back of the farm. This time his little legs didn't stop until he'd reached his favourite and secluded refuge where like many young lads in times of stress he withdrew into himself, wandering beside the stream, climbing the gnarled trees that were his own world, and watching the wild life there was then in abundance.

Of course after a while his parents began to worry and when it became late the whole family started a search of the boy's haunts for him. Young Bob wasn't slow to learn that sympathy could be gained out of concern when he was in trouble, thus taking the edge off any forthcoming rebuke.

Once whilst waiting at Frogs Hole for the Rolling's store lorry to take them to school one of the other lads had angered Bob and they'd had a set to during which Bob boxed the other lad's ears. Of course when the boy got home he told his mum who duly supplied him with a note to take to the head teacher Mr Cleary the next day. This boy however made the error of waving it in Bob's face the next morning saying how it was going to get him into trouble. This was a fatal mistake; for Bob snatched the note from him tore it into little pieces and trampled it into the mud before boxing the lad's ears yet again. After a repeat performance the following morning the boy's mother had had enough and appeared in person to ensure that this time it was Bob who took a beating indignant that schoolboy justice had not prevailed.

Although in those days the idea of school meals didn't have

the same orderly organisation as in later years it did exist in rural areas. At Benenden they had a building referred to as the Cadugan building annexed to the school and it was here that those pupils not able to go home for dinner went for their lunch.

One of Bob's friends was a boy named Jack Miller who in later years was to have a watch repair shop in Tenterden. This day the menu amongst other things included jacket potatoes [called baked spuds in those days] and they, the potatoes, were left out on a serve yourself basis. The idea that these hot soft round as a boys hand vegetables might make ideal missiles seemed to enter both boy's minds at once for there ensued a memorable battle in the Cadugan building that day, the soft potatoes bursting on impact causing a cleaner's nightmare in the process.

Once the ammunition was used up and the teachers arrived to restore order Jack and Bob were identified for a caning. But as Jack later revealed he had stolen the teacher's canes before hand and the punishment was left as a severe admonishment.

Bob rarely avoided the cane. He was caned for his escapade with the shot gun cartridges in the classroom stove, so the battle of Cadugan was a real victory for them.

One day in class Bob dropped his pencil and on stooping to pick it up noticed the school mistress Maggie Baker was sat with her legs apart *[days without modesty panels]* and to his schoolboy delight the colour of her knickers. He noticed also that they were in fact unlike ordinary girlie knickers but drawn together just above the knee, indeed they were bloomers or more accurately drawers, a more common garment in those days. Elastic round the legs elastic round the waist and so he christened them Mrs Maggie Baker's 'Harvest festival drawers' on the basis that 'all was safely gathered in.'

But this initial observation didn't end there for Bob was to make a habit of this inspection and in true scientific obedience carefully noted the colour each and every day until he and his brother Michael were able to publish the results of the research for the amusement of the class; Monday blue, Tuesday brown, Wednesday black and so on.

Needless to say he was found out and received the stick yet again.

There was a short period in young Bob's life when he was forced by circumstance to live with his grandmother at Priory Mead Biddenden and this of course meant a change of schools. The reason for this change was that his father old Bob had struck a horse whilst riding his motor cycle and become incapacitated. So it was that Bob went to Biddenden School where he met a lad who was to become his life long friend. A boy by the name of Dick Offen.

Dick actually went to school on donkey and cart, which was tied to the railings of the school until at dinner break he'd charge a ha-penny for rides across the playground. Unsurprisingly Dick was to become a farmer, dealer, and entrepreneur.

Readers of John Steinbeck will recall the Hamilton Family in East of Eden and how Tom took out his pocket knife and cut the membrane under the tongue of his pretty sister Mollie to cure her speech impediment.

That sort of courage is rare, especially in a child, and inhibited mostly by either fear or ignorance. Young Bob had that sort of courage.

He had had the misfortune to shoot his brother in the thumb with his air rifle and Michael whose misfortune it really was hugged the bloody appendage to his chest as he made for home.

Bob persuaded his brother to let him have a look and there glistening somewhere deep in the fleshy part of his thumb was the point 22 super dome lead pellet.

Taking out his pocket knife Bob, after some resistance from Michael, took hold of his brother's hand and cut out the slug. Bob knew his father would box his ears if he was found out and made his brother swear on pain of a beating if he told. No one will ever know if the operation was the result of courage or fear of the consequences.

The incident with the air rifle had followed on in the boy's lives from having bows and arrows to slings and catapults, a sort of natural progression. The next stage, though much later in life, was the proud ownership of a four-ten rim fire double barrelled pistol. A rare animal indeed, the meat and drink of bank robbers, but this was not a sawn off shotgun. There was no point, in young Bob's mind, in having a gun if it couldn't be fired, so fire it he did at arms length like in the films. Bob had reckoned without the recoil, indeed he'd perhaps not experienced such a thing and clearly forgotten that Newton's law say's that every action has a reaction. The recoil was swift following the explosion, and almost simultaneously, throwing the short barrels back into his face.

The shock was the worst thing, the unexpected whack on his nose and forehead, followed by the warm trickle of blood and the salty taste. His mother however was even more shocked. She had heard the shot, moved quickly outside to investigate, to see with horror her son's face covered in blood, believing for minutes he had shot himself.

Undeterred Bob thought perhaps he might persuade his mates to try it too, indeed squinting through his two black eyes he was heard to say he felt like Wyatt Earp until he pulled the bloody trigger; understandably there were no takers. Not much was seen of the four-ten after that.

Bob often got into scrapes with the other lads and had his ears boxed for it, probably twice if his father found out. In later years hardly an evening's football commentary went by on the TV without Bob remarking [in a somewhat endearing way] of how he boxed the ears of Brian Moore a schoolboy adversary at the same school.

In 1944 when the last day of his school life arrived the head teacher took the school leavers aside and gave them all a pep talk, passing on little nuggets of advice to them, dwelling perhaps on their weaknesses and their strengths preparing them for the outside world. When he came to Young Bob he threw up his arms and said. 'Bob Luck I have never been able to do anything with you and doubt very much if anyone ever will.' And with that his school days at Benenden were over.

Maidstone Market

Bob hadn't left school without prospects despite the Head master's opinion of him as it must have been obvious to those who knew of him through experience, bad or otherwise, that a lad with such spunk was bound to go forward.

His father, old Bob, was sure he would make a good farmer, and under his strict supervision his education started with a trip to Maidstone market. It was here old Bob decided his son would have his own pen of store pigs as his first responsibility and not only that, the lad would bid for them himself. Well not exactly, not at fourteen years old, but the idea was he would take notice of the auctioneer, get the feel of the market proper, understand the double talk and actually make the bid. Old Bob told him to go and stand behind the auctioneer and when ever his father wanted to bid he would signal his son. His son's instructions however were to pinch the auctioneer's bum to signify his bid. It is easy at this early juncture to see where the mischievous increment of young Bob's nature came from. However the upshot was, that not only did he get a strong eye from the auctioneer during the proceedings as he tried to brush away the little lad behind him, but the lad also managed to buy a pen of pigs. It wasn't until they asked young Bob his name and questions like, who are you with and how old are you? It was then that his father winked at the Auctioneer and the whole plan unfolded.

If old Bob ever wondered where his son inherited his addiction to practical jokes he shouldn't have, for it doesn't take much for anyone to realise it was a case of like father like son. Old Bob would wander around Maidstone market with a pocket full of dried peas dropping them down the Wellington's of his unsuspecting peers and with the youngster by his side this sort of fun was always going to rub off. Seeing local farmers hopping about on one leg shaking out their wellies in the middle of a busy market was after all country humour. Such things as his father's dribbling glass and the plastic dog faeces were what you might call 'bought in' jokes but young Bob was to become more an opportunist joker. As a grown adult he tied a fox's brush to his mother-in-law's coat tail and off she walked out of the Vine Pub and down Tenterden high street oblivious of the attachment. Of course good taste never came into the equation as taste is a state of mind and he knew, most times, when he could get away with things. He knew Glad, his mother-in-law, wouldn't have been too mad about the fox's brush as it was done out of spontaneous mischief, after all he respected her for a lot, not least of all her ability to set snares, no not fox wires, but snares for rabbits at which she could expertly read the runs and peg out the loops one hand high, like, she may have said, a real country girl should. Evelyn relates that during the war her mother would cook as many as 12 rabbits a week baked, roast, stewed or under a pie crust, the family then was seven, grandfather, mum, dad, Evelyn, her sisters and brother. In these days of CV's full of GCE's there's few children nowadays who were ever ferreting before they could walk as Evelyn was with her mother, and little if any will recognise a rabbit without its skin. Lots of country lore disappeared with Glad's generation as it was to with Bob's. Who? Bob might ask, has used the sugar bag trick since the demise of the old blue sugar bag? The old one pound blue sugar bag just fitted over a pheasants head half way down the neck of the bird. If you put some maize in the bottom of it, some molasses [yeah okay treacle] around the inside of the rim then stood it in the stubble you'd catch yourself a pheasant. How? The birds reached into the bag and the bag stuck over their head, and, like the cap on a falcon it was roosting time already. Try it.

It was just before Young Bob was sent off to the Kent Farm Institute in 1947 that on a visit to Tenterden Fair, as Tenterden stock market was known, he was helping herd some calves along the high street having brought them in from the country to sell. Herding or droving isn't the easiest of jobs and never as easy as the halcyon summer shots we have seen of primitive people followed obediently by fifty or so long eared sheep, or long horn cows even, often to the musical accompaniment of tiny bells. No this was Tenterden market town as it was then, traffic was on the increase and they had half a dozen frisky bull calves to move along the narrow bit of road just after the old Tollgate.

It just happened that the wine shop door *[Victoria as it is now]* had been left open as shop doors often were on fine days, and whereas most beasts would want to trot along the open part of the road one particular calf went straight into the shop.

Not withstanding the dilemma of having eleven calves running ahead and one in a shop with only young Bob and his father to cope, but the one in the shop got wedged behind the counter. Wedged is the operative word as the counter space was limited by crates and bottles, not so many cans in those days, but row upon row of corks of chateaux this and that providing enough friction against the tough hide of the already frightened beast to cause a big problem. The bottles rattling, the beast bellowing and young Bob shouting, frightened the proprietor into the back shop until eventually the animal was turned around and high tailed it out of the shop doorway. Remarkably there was no damage, to the animal anyway, but there were, no doubt, people saying in the market that day, *'of all the calves to head for the wine shop it had to be Bob Luck's'* or *'perhaps it could smell the cider and thought he was 'ome already!'*.

Young Bob and Evelyn were coming home from Haywards Heath market on one occasion having acquired some new calves when passing through one of the villages the rear doors of the lorry came undone and the calves jumped out. Fortunately young Bob was alive to what was happening and stopped the lorry. Rounding up the calves proved to be quite strenuous for them both and they were just wrestling with the last obstinate beast when a lady who had been watching over her garden hedge said rather sternly.

'Hey you. Wot yer doin ter that poor animal?

Bob whose physical effort with the last of the 3cwt calves, made him red faced with the exertion, and absolutely angry with himself for not making sure they were secure, was just about on his knees. Absolutely exasperated with the woman's remark, he said with untypical calm.

'Just giving the little buggers a bit of exercise missus that's wot I'm doin!'

Horses, Ponies and Traps etc.

About the time Young Bob left school a friend of old Bob's by the name of Frank Witherden lived at Hoadsbrook Farm Benenden on the opposite side to the Hospital, a sanatorium in those days. Well, Frank was a horsy hunting type of chap and knowing the lad was built sparse like a jockey and had an affinity with horses suggested to his parents they send him down to Tom Masson at Lewes to train as one. But old Bob would have none of it fearing his son might break too many bones.

Evelyn has a picture of Bob riding his daughter's little pony and one of him on a *'bloomin great'* hunter taken in about 1997. But despite his love of the animals he never could take to riding.

Bob's grandfather who farmed at High Lees near Beltring was a regular user of the pony and trap just as young Bob was and indeed as to this day is young Bob's Widow, Evelyn.

Tragically Bob's grandfather and his expectant wife were tipped out of the trap when something startled the pony. The trap passed over them both, leaving young Bob's grandfather in a paraplegic state to pass away after about nine years. Happily this accident did not affect his wife's pregnancy for she eventually gave birth to a daughter, young Bob's Aunt Vera.

Although Bob couldn't ride, horses and ponies figure in his family's life in many respects. As has already been recounted his father old Bob collided with a gypsy's horse which was asleep in the middle of the road. He whilst riding on his motor cycle when travelling through Small Hythe killing the horse and putting himself in hospital for a period leaving the need to re-house young Bob with his granny, Flo Luck at Priory Mead near Woolpack corner.

Bob and Evelyn with their Pony and Trap
Church Road, Tenterden

It's been said young Bob didn't ride but he was already a jockey in his head with a great love of horses and the sport of Kings; always quite keen on having a bet. It was whilst on his way to Charing Point-to-Point races he fell off his friend's John Jefferys' motor cycle at the notorious Gascoigne's corner at High Halden. We're told he bounced up the road like a rubber ball, rubbed himself down, remounted in good equestrian fashion, and went on to see his horse Baffin Bay come home at twenty five to one. It seems he couldn't stay on a motor cycle either.

Always ready to hitch a ride to the races Jim Thompson's motor cycle this time and another year at Charing.. This time there was the well known tipster Prince Monolulu waiting for the punters as they came onto the course. He was a very colourful character, African origin, lovely wide smile and a flamboyant dresser especially his head-dress which was mainly ostrich feathers. Young Bob succumbed to his patter and bought a few tips from him. Of course having paid for the tips Bob kept them to himself and backed accordingly. The first race came up at good odds and Bob splashed the lot on the next horse which also romped home. Life hadn't been so lucky for Bob in a long time as still the horses kept winning; doubles and trebles weren't really his scene but this day he was rolling in it. Along came the last race and Bob was all set to put the lot on it when his brother Michael fearful he was bound to lose told him he'd be mad to do so. Going against his nature Bob saw his brother's reason and made just a modest bet... the horse romped home.

There were no recriminations, Bob's pockets were full of white fivers anyway; he didn't know how much, he didn't care how much. He called it bookies money, as though it wasn't really his. On the way home they all stopped for a drink at a pub in Pluckley where Bob counted his winnings stopping somewhere in the hundreds. That evening Bob invited Jim Thompson, Don Clark, Ray Millen and his brother Michael to meet him at the White Lion where he bought them all a slap-up meal and no doubt a modest drink or two.

He was less lucky on another occasion when he went to

the Epsom derby with a coach load from the Tenterden Club. The race course toilets in those days were utilitarian if not down right rustic, built in the manner of most country fairs by placing six posts around a trench and tacking on Hessian for the sake of privacy.

Of course the beer tent was, logically, not too far away and towards the end of the meet conditions were to say the least, slippery underfoot. Bob, never the steadiest on his feet at these times lost his footing and ended up in the trench.

Bob had some good friends in the Tenterden Working Men's club as it was then called; indeed he was later to become an honorary life member. None would ever have deserted him in times of real need but; he smelled like a sewer and no way would he be allowed on the coach. Unless he wanted to walk home he had to go round the tents and stalls and buy new trousers and footwear. Whether it can be said he was lucky on the course that day must be left to conjecture.

Nothing to do with the name, indeed one might say people make their own luck by their nature and attitude to life. Bob regarded himself as lucky in life as well as on the course. He backed the outsider Foinavon when it won the national in '67.

This affinity to horses and the country clings to young Bob throughout his life; how strange that before he married his wife Evelyn; indeed she would be about sixteen years old when her parents decided she had out-grown the dapple grey pony she rode with distinction at many a gymkhana throughout Kent.

She was bought to her great surprise and pride a thoroughbred filly, the Sire of which was called ***Robert Barker*** and the dam called ***Stolen Love.*** The owners chose to use these names to create the new registered name for the foal, taking ***Robert*** from the sire and ***Love*** from the dam. Uncanny that her future husband should be Robert [Young Bob] and that her thoroughbred horse be called all things **'*Robert's Love*'**. Remarkable.

Evelyn Luck with Silver Shadow

The mare 'Robert's Love' stable name was Stardust and to Evelyn's chagrin her father-in-law old Bob wouldn't allow her to keep it at Goodshill when she later married young Bob and so the mare was sold-on. Most animal lovers feel a wrench at having to let go of a creature they have come to love and it was natural that Evelyn should keep track of the horse. The mare eventually was settled with a Mrs Hunt from Sparsholt near Winchester, having previously been with a Mr Sergeant from Saltwood at Hythe. She was registered in the general Stud book and became a brood mare.

Now it so happened that ***Tom Griffiths*** the race horse trainer who had trained the filly as a two year old took over the Carpenter's Arms Pub at Mayfield in Sussex and the Carpenter's Arms was a good client for 'Bob Luck Cider' so it was easily one of their more looked forward to deliveries; Perhaps a pub lunch a drop to drink and a good old chin-wag about racing.

The mare was first put to the stallion ***Indigenous*** to produce a foal named Native Copper. Later she was put to the stallion ***Pinza*** on which ***Sir Gordon Richards*** won the 1953 Derby trained by Noel Murless. She returned to ***Pinza*** twice more and all the foals were national hunt winners.

Visits to the Carpenter's Arms were regular and as it was a real Sport of Kings pub it was frequented by jockeys such as ; ***Geordie Ramshaw, R.P. [Bobbie] Elliot,*** and ***Geof Lewis*** *[still training to this day]* all were attached to ***Tom Griffiths.***

When these jockeys, then household names, heard in the pub one night that Evelyn and young Bob were to marry or as one of them put it , Bob was '*taking on a young filly*' their advice was; '*Hold her head up high and give her a good kick in the ribs!*' But it was Bob that was to be later kicked in the ribs.

Smarden: Working for Uncle Sid - 1944

When Bob finished school he was sent to work for his Uncle Sid at Homersham farm Smarden. His Uncle had a few hop gardens and also some livestock, sheep and cattle. Homersham Farm is situated on the flat vale of land that stretches from Smarden to Egerton in the North and this land was exactly what was needed during these war years for our Fighter Command. In 1943 vast tracts of it were commandeered for the construction of an air field.

There were two runways each about 1200 yards long. One ran east west and the other north south both wide enough for the Spitfires of the Canadian 421 & 403 squadrons to scramble four abreast.

To facilitate the North-South runway several ponds had to be filled in and farm buildings including an Oast House had to be demolished at the southern end.

By the time young Bob arrived at his Uncle Sid's, he like all boys of fourteen were mad about aircraft. Most of these lads could tell the type, make, speed, ammunition even, almost as well as the observation corps situated at strategic places around the South east.

In his free time Bob would have walked only two hundred yards to be at the south end of the runway, to see the Ack ack positions dug in all around and to watch the aircraft coming home.

By 1944 RAF heroes like John Edgar Johnson and his famous Black Labrador were no longer to be seen wandering around the country lanes and neither were the aerobatics of George 'screwball' Beurling as now the American 362 Fighter Squadron had arrived with their flashy insignia and shark painted Thunderbolt Fighter planes.

It is easy to see the fascination young Bob would have, as

every day he would have aircraft for company. He often related to Evelyn in vivid detail of seeing the badly shot-up Flying Fortresses forced to land on these short airstrips for want of fuel and later to feel the consequences of the Thunderbolt which ran out of runway to finally demolish Southerden Farm Oast on June7th 1944.

Whereas young Bob at fourteen was working away from home and getting his first taste of farm work right in the middle of an operational fighter squadron; building on tales of war to relate one day to his wife Evelyn. Evelyn was little more than five years old yet had imprinted in her young mind a memory of her own, for one day living as she then did at Heronden the family was about to sit down to their dinner. Grandfather was lying on the couch beneath the living room window and the table was laid in preparation for the meal when her father heard the unmistakable sound of a doodlebug. Evelyn's sister Joan who was then just a toddler was outside in the sun. Evelyn was told to get under the kitchen table and to stay there, her mother dashing outside to bring her sister inside. Their haste would have been insufficient to avert danger as the doodlebug quickly passed over, hotly pursued by a fighter plane trying to turn the enemy bomb around. The spectacle however wasn't to be missed and mother, father and the recovered infant Joan paused to watch them disappearing over the marshes. The delay of her mother's return and the lonely feeling sitting under the kitchen table was too much for Evelyn who scrambled outside to join them, followed at a more leisurely pace by Grandfather who paused halfway down the garden path to light a cigarette.

By now the two aircraft were distant objects and it was just as the party turned that a second doodlebug skimmed the rooftops and exploded with an horrendous explosion in the cornfield behind the house three hundred yards distant. The shock wave tugged at their clothes and whipped through the house breaking the windows and collapsing the ceilings. Evelyn remembers seeing the oil lamps that hung above the table smashed among the food, and the settee Grandpa had been sitting on moment before covered with glass. Amazingly the tough old man standing as he was before the house was unhurt save to complain about the loss of the cigarette he'd just lit. Evelyn remembers the explosion set fire to the standing crop of corn and the local brigade had to be called to put it out.

At Uncle Sid's the consequences of losing another Oast house with a standing crop of hops only two months away from picking posed real problems to a farmer. Okay not so bad as having Hitler coming across the channel but problems nevertheless. Of course growers like Bob's Uncle Sid would all muck in to share the drying and there is no doubt this is where Bob learned the drying trade.

Learners however must be attentive and to this adolescent already developing the signs of a mischief maker; attention was not given easily. One day when his inattentiveness had graduated to downright trouble making he was warned by the Palmer brothers, neighbours of his uncle Sid's, to get on with his work and cut out the mischief, but alas the effects of his 'telling off' lasted no more than an hour. The frustration of the two older men manifested itself into a threat that young Bob would lose his trousers if he did not behave himself. In later more mature years on, young Bob would learn to read peoples faces and body language like no other, but now he was at fourteen, half man half boy, as far as he was concerned mischief made the world go round and they, the other workers, couldn't mean it, they were too busy anyway.

How wrong he was. Frank Palmer's patience broke and young Bob was ensnared with the help of Jack Offen somewhere in the oast house, roughly debagged and his trousers taken half a mile away and thrown into Crump's orchard across the Smarden road.

The indignity of crossing the Smarden road, 'sans culotte' or 'bare arsed' call it what you will, to look for his trousers in Crumps orchard was a lesson young Bob never forgot.

Hop Drying

After picking, the hops were measured by the bushel from the bins and put into large yellow coloured Hessian sack called Pokes. Each poke usually held ten bushels and they were transported to the Oast where thirty or forty pokes were required for an Oasting. The Oast house consisted of a high level floor in a large roundel built over a kiln. The floor was covered with a strong horse hair mat onto which the hops were spread. The internal area of the roundel was reached by way of steps onto a landing six to eight feet above the first floor level.

It was the hop driers job to spread the hops level using his feet to get underneath them walking on the hair mat so as not to crush the valuable crop, often he would use a wooden rake to spread the hops evenly as he moved around the roundel.

At the base of the Oast ground floor a tunnel stretched the length of the kiln. Either side of the tunnel were four evenly spaced fire alcoves. The fires were set about 18" above the floor on large iron fire baskets. The fires were started with large pieces of charcoal and then sustained by anthracite [Welsh Coal]. The heat rose from the fires through the kiln up to the drying room floors above. In order to preserve the colour of the hops, rolled sulphur commonly known as brimstone was burned in a special shallow pan-like device near the kiln. The whole process took about eight hours during which time the hops had to be continually inspected and if necessary turned again to make sure they dried evenly.

The drying process commenced once they had the required load on the drying room floor and the dryer himself lived with the crop day and night having a makeshift bed near the kiln. As soon as the crops were dried he would use a shovel-like tool called a Scuppit to move the hops off the hair mat into the cooling room floor. When the hops were cool they were scuppited through a trap into a large jute sack called a Pocket held in place by a metal hoop. A press was turned by hand and the circular head of the press pressed each successive load down into the pocket until the load was full, tight and weighing about one and a half hundredweight [168lbs].

A webbing sling allowed the pocket to be raised so that the opening could be stitched up; a procedure called 'coping'.

By the time the pressing was finished there would be another load ready for drying so the hop dryer and his mate had little time for themselves. Towards the end of a week the ash pits of the fires were so full that baked potatoes made a change from the dry fare of sandwiches and were said to be traditionally better than any other baked potatoes.

Each pocket was stencilled with the owners/producers name, farm name, numbered, and dated, before being sent off to the 'Hop Marketing Board in London.

Kent Farm Institute 1947-48

The Kent farm institute was a source of higher education for those moving towards a career or lively-hood on the land. It was held in the old grammar school building in Riddles road Sittingbourne with an annexed place for practical learning at Grove Farm Tunstall.

Young Bob attended the General Agriculture course from September 1947 until July 1948 opting not to do the Fruit Growing Course held at the same College. Fellow course members recall the principal was a Mr Robert Hart and the lecturers Mr Cameron [Management] Mr Butler, and Mr Dutt .[Entomology] the class sizes were around thirty or so with the larger proportion being recently demobbed service men. Young minds remember what aroused their sense of fun and the warden was one such gentleman, yes Mr Allden was remembered endearingly as Allden the Warden *[with sometimes the affix 'the sod!']*. More endearingly perhaps was the secretary Ms Nicholson who was, apparently, so well endowed she was worth watching on the tennis courts.

Bob at this stage was only seventeen and of course the younger course members came in for closer guardianship than the mature students. If Bob wanted to get out in the evenings for a trip down to the local pub *[he was under age]* he had to break out of College via the roof of his room. On one such occasion he had returned from the pub with some of the other lads, shinned up the wall onto the roof, along the roof and in through the window to find to his horror and embarrassment the school Principle sat on his bed. It was a fair cop and a good wigging was what he got for his absence.

Bob and his friends were returning to College from a Saturday evening in one of the local hostelries. Their route took them through a rather nice housing estate, a sort of crescent of houses built around a circular island of grass.

Whose idea it was we shall never know but the idea of taking off the gates of the houses and piling them up on the island was Bob's sort of fun and they set about it with the gusto given them by the evening's alcohol. They had removed several gates when:-

'Where do you think you are going with that?' The policeman demanded. With the gate on his shoulders Bob could no doubt only see the constable's boots but the recognition was clear enough. Turning around he shouted over his shoulder. *'Back again officer!'*

The group got their *'telling off'* there in the darkness of the evening probably swaying gently and trying to look suitably ashamed. It was sometime later when Bob responded to a call for volunteers for the Tug O War team to play for the College against a selection of teams including a team from the Maidstone Police. Who should be in the opposing team but the same Constable from the gate lifting evening? It was a very dark night; Bob consoled himself, but not that dark apparently. *'Hey I know you don't I?'* The big burly Copper shouted. *'You're the "just going back again man" aren't you?'*

Bob was nonplussed in front of his mates, some asking what was all that about. No way could he leave the line, standing with his bit of rope ready as they were to pull for the College. But the big policeman was off duty and anyway there was a glimmer of a smile his eyes. *'Sorry'* Bob grinned and the rest of the day went off without a hitch

Bob completed his education in the ways of agriculture at the institute and left his mark there for others to remember him, even if only by participating in the hunger strike for of all things more food and eating a whole box of grapefruit to keep the hunger pangs at bay. Then there was the wager won against eating a slice of bread liberally covered with mustard and last but not least by changing their postal address to 'Piddles Road'.

Shooting & Foxes

Country Things 1950's

Young Bob was, first and foremost, a countryman. Farm bred from generations of farmers. It was his Father, old Bob who started the cider business in 1935 starting the trend away from the land if only obliquely, as apples and 'cider making' are very much the cusp between commerce and farming.

Being a Countryman he was never far away from the husbandry of the land, and foxes figured largely in that way. Not only were they still the pest they are today but the movement against the use and wearing of fur had not yet begun and in those days their pelts were of some value, [£10 in 1980] and were sent to NECCI Bros at Staplehurst for processing before being sent to Germany.

Evelyn recalls the day when foxes were such a pest they came up to the farm in broad daylight to try take her bantams and only a word around the family friends to make a shoot of it, resolved the problem.

[NB: On the morning of this being written Evelyn who now keeps chickens for her livelihood had to ring the local farmer to come and shoot a fox caught in a fox trap less than twenty yards from the chicken house. She knew the fox had been in the trap all night as her terriers had being going berserk to get out. By the time the farmer arrived the fox had escaped the trap. 2002-12-04]

The trap in question was built for Evelyn by her son-in-law Robert, Julie's husband. Bob had remarked that he would eat his hat if a fox was ever caught *'in that bloody contraption!'* and was reminded repeatedly thereafter of his rash promise as the trap hadn't failed in all the years between until 2002. But he never ate his hat.

Left to Right: Bob Luck with Dodger. Brian Martin. George Babbage. John Hook. Peter Johns. Butch Goodsell. Colin Day. John Day. Alan Day. Michael Hook with Whisky

Evelyn goes on to recall an evening at the Tenterden club when Bob was having a jar with friends and the hunting was being debated at some length. The appropriately named Gerry Hunt then president of the Tenterden Club and, some say, a townie! *[which is not an insult, but refers more to incomers with little country knowledge.]* Well, a group of them were discussing the bag at some recent fox drive and Gerry's brother was expounding the virtues of the urban fox as against its rural cousin and perhaps, it must be said, that his audience were either too polite or too far into their cups to contradict his theory. Now, at the point where the speaker was extolling the superb and much more refined features of the urban fox and describing in detail its beautiful and extra long nose when Bob who had just about had enough of it interjected. *'Aye that's right.'* Of course Gerry beamed at the idea that they had Bob's support, after all wasn't Bob's name revered in country knowledge. However, this feeling of euphoria was short lived, for Bob followed up his remark with a mocking. *'And wot's more you can see that little turned up snout they have for lifting off the dustbin lids!'*

The Brann's the Luck's the Clarke's and the Bignell's:

That the four families were inextricably linked through the nearness of geography and trade wasn't uncommon in those early country days. The Bignell's owned a fish shop in Tenterden and the Clarke's came to farm Heronden from Benenden. The Luck's and the Brann's shared marches in Wittersham, having Acton and Poplar farms so these generations and their children shared the same farming environment; the same country beginnings. It was within this country environment that young Bob was beginning to build a reputation; many saw him as a joker like his father, through learned behaviour perhaps they would argue, more saw him as a countryman and a few as a rebel, but to paint this picture of him was confounded frequently by acts of sensitivity. At the age of twelve Evelyn then a Bignell, remembers an incident on the shoot after a drive down through Gazedown wood, her grandfather's place. A cock bird was shot and landed in deep water. The spaniel sent in to retrieve it got stuck in the fork of a submerged willow and was on the verge of being lost. Whereas no one would or should risk his own life, even for his own dog, here on this occasion young Bob strips off his clothes to swim out into the water to rescue someone else's drowning spaniel.

Jack Russell *[the man not the dog]* who used to work for Evelyn's grandfather at the time took off his old army great coat, rubbed Bob down with it and Bob was soon dressed and back on with the shoot

Bob and one of his mates were often asked by his father out to the bleak and inhospitable Isle of Sheppey to shoot, Sheppey being, then and to this day, a great venue for incoming wild fowl; Days when one hid up and waited for a flight of birds to come in to feed. Teal and Widgeon flying really high, birds that would wheel around and go back if they saw any ground movement, when, Bob would say today, shooting was fair and the birds you hit were hard won.

Well, they had their shots and two good hard hit birds fell on the other side of the fleet. Now for those who don't know

Sheppey, a fleet is a salt water drainage channel, often very deep and fifteen to twenty yards wide. To make matters interesting there was a covering of ice too. Bob's brother Michael immediately wrote off the two birds, after all, they didn't have a dog with them that could make the retrieve, they weren't into gun dogs, theirs were terriers, and what's more, there was no bridge for more than a mile. Not so Bob. He wasn't going to leave those hard won birds to the foxes, without more than a brief look at the water he stripped off to his skin and, breaking the ice with his arms, swam across the fleet went over the marsh and retrieved the two birds and swam back. He then quickly dressed in front of the astounded onlookers fished out a bottle of rum, took a few swigs and carried on as if that was the norm.

Bob and one of his mates were into the art of long netting which is about the easiest, some say laziest form of picking up rabbits. If you can put out your long nets late afternoon stretched across the runs, the rabbits can be pushed into the nets with very little noise and the nets dropped on them. It's a sort of dry land purse net fishing if you like. You only need to walk up rattle a match box now and then and they're yours. Except it does not always go to plan and the nets aren't cheap. Bob and his mate had the misfortune to lay out their net one time when unknown to them the farmer had let a flock of ewes into the same field. When they came back after dark Bob and co unwittingly drove the sheep into the nets and the sheep being strong beasts and prone to just a bit of panic to say the least, cost them their cherished equipment. Of course there were no rabbits that night.

Young Bob was invited by his father to go partridge shooting on some land Sittingbourne way. The land happened to be nearly all orchards and in particular pear orchard grown on espalier trained trees in very narrow rows. This manner of planting left very little visibility but there was, they reasoned, no danger provided they kept a decent line with the other guns, a good rule when walking up on game.

When the two, father and son, came out of the orchard some time later they could hardly get a word in edgeways as each struggled to complain to the other about some bugger in the line shooting low. *'Look at this!'* said young Bob and he pulled the shirt out of his trousers, pellets pinging off him as he did so; the shirt fabric had been the only thing preventing the shot breaking the skin. *'Yeah! You think that's bad'* said his Dad. His father did the same sending out a little shower of pellets too. Both had been next to one another in the line less than forty yards away, neither would openly admit they may have had a low shot, but both privately would chuckle about the day they peppered the other.

Such was his reputation young Bob was often called out to deal with fox problems and would respond anywhere with his gun and the terriers. It was about 1978 when he had a call from the Morris's of Haylands Farm Smarden to say they had a serious problem and that a family of foxes were about. It was Evelyn who took the call that Sunday lunch time as she recalls setting aside the Sunday lunch preparations to go and call Bob who had taken the gun up the field. Evelyn met him on the way back with his gun over one shoulder and a dog fox over the other.

'We've a job on' she said, advising him of the telephone message, so off they went with their three Jack Russell terriers Whisky, Shandy and the seven month old puppy Dodger. On arrival at the farm they were directed towards the nearby wood. Evelyn had hardly stepped over the wire into the wood with the three dogs at her heels when she surprised the two adult foxes and raised the alarm. Holding back the young dog she urged the other terriers after them, of course they needed no second telling and soon chased through the wood as far as small culvert which they entered without hesitation.

Bob had seen what was happening from the field and rushed to other end of the culvert to shoot both adults and five cubs as they emerged. Now it must be said that to a townie these facts related in cold blood simply stoke up legions of abhorrence, the killing of a family of foxes Mum Dad and the kids so to speak, but it has to be recognised the potential killing power of seven foxes, the damage they can do if allowed. Their deaths were quick, humane and legal. What is more; to a country man that was a smart piece of shooting because the twelve bore shotgun only holds two shots so Bob *'the expert'* had to reload twice in a matter of seconds, no mean feat.

The story does not end there for one of the Morris brothers called out *'don't go yet there's another one in the chicken house.'* He'd wondered why the chickens wouldn't go in and had a look inside to find another cub in there. This too was duly dispatched bringing the total to eight plus the one he'd shot before the phone call making a bag of nine in one day.

Fox litters aren't usually as large as six and it was clear to Evelyn that because the litter was so large the dog Fox had stayed behind to help the Vixen who, remarkably, had lost one of her back legs above the hock, perhaps in a combine she surmised. Students of nature will know the dog fox usually clears off when the litter arrives if indeed he's not sent away by the Vixen.

Graham Saunders Relates

Young Bob was actually bitten by a fox. Bob was asked out to Dennis Clifton's place, Court Lodge Farm and was with

Young Bob with a Fox
Left: Gordon Tompsett – Right: Harold Winter

Cyril Saunders and Arthur Freeman who worked on the next farm for Lord Nunburnholme. They hadn't been digging the earth long when they reached the fox and Bob told Cyril to hold back the terriers. Bob reached in for the fox and as soon as he drew it out it turned short and bit him through the arm. Of course there was no holding it after that but Arthur had his gun and shot it dead before it got too far, they shot two others that day.

On another day Graham and Bob were out on Dungeness Beach when Bob saw and shot a fox, but only wounded it, although Bob was walking with a stick because of his hip problem he still picked up the fox swung it over his head and killed it on the beach.

It's hard to say if these actions are brave, cruel, foolhardy or what. Bob could have expended another cartridge to put the fox to sleep, but he was upon it before he realised it wasn't dead and putting the animal down in this seemingly risky or barbaric fashion made no difference to the outcome.

Badgers have been protected for some years now and

Left to Right: Harold Martin. Maurice Beeslee. Cyril Moore. Jim Sims. Bert Martin. Cliff Marshall. Bob Luck. Unknown. Unknown. Kneeling Unknown. Dog, Vicky 1.

their populations are, in 2003, reaching uncomfortable proportions. This wasn't always the case, once a keeper's gibbet would often display a dead badger or two along with the corvids and other, so called, vermin, now things have changed for now even game keepers are a threatened species.

In the sixties it was never an easy mistake to send your dog into a sett and claim it was an earth, no self respecting countryman would admit he didn't know the difference, but as has been said before, the fox and the badger are known to sometimes share the same earth works. Sometimes you didn't know. Anyone that values his dogs wouldn't back them against an angry sett of badgers and so it was never deliberate. But this day it did happen and when Bob got his dog back he was asked how he knew he was wrong. He replied quietly: '*Cos the little bitch came up with a mouthful of shaving brushes, that's why.*' Bob had a turn of phrase second to none where expression was concerned. [NB: Wet shaving brushes were always made from the pale guard hairs taken from badger fur.]

Because badgers are a protected species doesn't take them from the country scene, indeed whereas vermin can be removed if a nuisance, badgers have to be worked around. Dairy farmers blame them for carrying bovine tuberculosis and there are measures being taken in the West Country to try to establish the truth of this issue. Young Bob was always in tune with nature and was the first to admire and respect these creatures; they are after all nocturnal animals and even country people don't get to see much of them. One evening when Evelyn and Bob were driving home to Millpond farm a badger dashed across the road in front of the car. '*There was nothing I could do to avoid the wretched thing, it just ran in front and I hit it.*' Evelyn stopped the car and Bob got out and ran round the back. He soon came back carrying a huge Boar badger. '*Just look at this big old bugger then!*' said Bob, holding a huge badger aloft by its back legs.

It was indeed one of the largest badgers either of them had ever seen. They admired it for a minute or two. The claws on the front legs measured two inches of hard curved nail, and the thick dark fur with its long grey guard hair was in prime condition. Between them they felt sorry for this creature so much like a bear yet actually a mustelid, cousin to the weasel family. This cuddly creature will kill hedgehogs, rabbits, fox cubs and have been known to raid poultry sheds. Normally they feed on fresh carrion, worms, wasp grubs, and roots.

'What you going to do with it then Bob?' Evelyn asked at last.

'Shove it in the boot then I can bury it in the morning.' He replied.

'Oh no, I don't think so Bob.' Evelyn was thinking of the times he'd said he would do something then forgotten, she didn't want a stinking Badger in the boot of her car. And it was stinking. As they stood there in the gathering darkness beside the road she could smell and hear the animal's scent glands working. *'You are sure its dead aren't you?'* Evelyn knew that badger's scent glands work overtime in times of stress, and sometimes after death. *'Best to leave it here then you can come back tomorrow and bury it alright Bob?*

Bob lay the giant down reverently besides the ditch and they continued homewards, thinking little more of the incident until the morning when Bob and she went out to bury it. The badger was nowhere to be seen. *'I thought you said it was dead Bob.'* Bob made to answer but before he could Evelyn continued. *'Well it couldn't have been could it? Just think of the mess the car would have been in with those claws of his when it came round. It was only stunned and you holding it up like that too!'*

In 1991 a neighbouring land owner called to complain that Evelyn's horses had got into their wheat crop and done a lot of damage and someone had better come and have a look as it was special long straw wheat grown for thatching. Of course it was a valuable crop and Bob took Evelyn along saying she'd better come as the horses were her business. When they got to the field they could see the damage wasn't due to horses but the gentleman insisted showing them what he thought were horse droppings.

'No,no, them's not horse droppings.' Bob didn't want to be

impolite, thinking neighbours are neighbours after all, and hadn't this bloke ever seen badger dung before. *'Look I'll show you.'* Bob lead the gentleman along the headland of the crop and found the badger's latrines, showed him the runs and where their fur had smoothed the clay, explained how the animals had decimated the field, rolled in it collected it for bedding, indeed the full nature talk.

At last the gentleman apologised, saying he'd no idea badgers made such a mess adding, no wonder the farmers down the West Country made such a fuss about them.

A Good Maxim

A good maxim for a shooting man might be 'make sure you have everything you need with you' because it might be a long walk back. Common sense you might say but it's not been unknown for handlers to arrive at field trials without their dogs. That's the 'cor blimey' maybe but forgetting cartridges is common. The Newmill Channel and the levels around it were always good for a few flights of duck. Of course in these days of four by four vehicles all your clobber and your dog can get almost anywhere. In the fifties things were different. A party of guns had got together to have a bit of sport on the marsh and to make life easier old Bob had asked Evelyn's grandfather Clarke for a loan of his fergie tractor and the dung cart, to take them all down onto the marsh in relative luxury. Young Bob was to drive the tractor.

It is important to understand the relative construction and uses of the dung cart. Because as the name implies its prime purpose was for muck spreading and therefore the means of loading and unloading had to be simple. It was a two wheel centre shafted cart of fairly high centre of gravity. The centre shaft, draw bar, *[or tinge bat as it was colloquially known]* was square in cross section and was joined to the tractor by sliding the shaft through a larger fixed box section aperture and held by a pin dropped into position from the top. Thus once the cart was loaded, to off-load it was simply done by pulling the pin and moving forward. This allowed the cart to tip up backwards off loading the muck.

We now live in a world of safety factors, safe working loads and a new EEC sort of ultra caution, but farm carts out-live the advance of technology and it's hard to say whether this cart was good for a ton or more or less; suffice to say there were nine in the shooting party.

Nine grown men averaging twelve stone is over fifteen hundred pounds, add to that their guns and their dogs, put them in an old dung cart and bounce them off down to the marshes does seem to forecast an interesting days shooting.

Young Bob was elected to drive and right from the outset he joked about pulling the pin out of the tinge bat such that those at the back worried that should this younger version of his notorious practical joker father ever dare; then they would be squashed by the others as the cart tipped over backwards. The front of the cart was therefore the safest place to be, but really none thought it would happen. And it didn't, not backwards anyway.

After a good days shooting the party loaded up again, dogs, men, guns and game all warm and comfy and satisfied with their day. No more the jokes of the outward trip, just to sit back and let the old fergie tractor pull them up the bank and back to Heronden.

By now it was very dark and it was at the first gateway, running with water off the channel, knee deep in slops, that young Bob stopped the tractor to wait for someone to open the gate. Whether the time had come for a new draw bar, tinge bar or cart-shaft, call it what you like, the tractor stopped, but the momentum imposed such energy upon it that it snapped tipping the cart forward not backwards, no one wanted to be at the back did they?

Those at the front were tipped unceremoniously out into the mud. Those at the middle fell forward onto those already fallen and last but not least the game birds dogs and those riding at the back rocketed onto the pile of seething splashing arms and legs amongst a mélange of game bags and cartridge cases. Epithets abounded and blued the air of the fog descending on the Newmill channel. Wrongly; their first thoughts, if not suspicions, were for the only spectator, young Bob bouncing gently on the sprung tractor seat, not knowing whether it was safe to laugh or not. *[Remember what Bateman said?]* Of course it is never safe for one person to laugh at the misfortunes of a crowd, especially if you've spent half the morning threatening to tip them out anyway.

Eventually the shooting party emerged from the mud. The considerable bulk of old Bob, Frank, Graham and Jack Saunders. Frank Spain and Peter Spain, Trevor

Collingwood and Frank Maylam.; Lord Nunburnholme his trademark bowler still firmly wedged on his head. One by one they unfastened themselves from one another. The dogs wagged their tails nervously as though this was some sort of new human game. It was moments before they all realised it was an accident. They were not after all going to have to hang young Bob in the nearest hop garden. It is not every day that nine humans five dogs, pheasants, ducks and guns are unceremoniously dumped in liquid mud, and for them all to come up unharmed and seeing the funny side of it.

Surprisingly no one was hurt, not a dog, not a gun was damaged after a day none of them will ever forget.

Gazedown wood and the banks and lanes around Heronden was a favourite place for Bob to take his gun for a few rabbits. This day he was out there with Evelyn's brother David. Wandering through the trees, Bob saw a rabbit and shot it, broke his gun and went to look for it. To his surprise up pops a lady carrying the rabbit. '*Here you are Bob, here's your rabbit, my love.*' She appeared as if by magic out of nowhere. Initially it all happened so casually they exchanged a few pleasantries and went on their way but then the shock hit him. What if he'd shot her? David never said there might be someone in the wood, but his father knew. Apparently in the late fifties primroses were picked, tied in bunches, and sent from Tenterden station up to London to be sold, every year they were a saleable crop and this lady had permission.

Young Bob was the first person people thought of when they had a fox problem. The administration at the Dungeness Bird Sanctuary had heard of Bob's reputation and contacted him to ask if he would do something about the alarming fox population at the sanctuary. They told Bob that they were worried that so many marauding foxes would decimate the ground nesting bird populations in the sanctuary. They were not talking game birds but summer gull populations, Sand pipers, Stone Curlews and the like; others much rarer birds too visiting the South East.

Bob's forays into the sanctuary became a regular feature of his shooting and he and his mates cleared the gravel dunes and shore scrub covered landscape of many foxes until they realised they were not the only ones invited onto the land. This realisation came about when a stranger shot one of Bob's mates dogs in the eye, the dog lived, but the question raised was obvious. Other groups, some inexperienced, no more than young lads, were roving about the dunes without a scrap of safety discipline, cocked hammer guns across their shoulders. Prudence dictated Bob would give Dungeness a miss after that.

Although foxes were enemy number one it was no use having a good pack of terriers and not doing a bit of ratting, so this too brought Bob out into farms and barns around this part of Kent. New plantations once wired off against rabbits had to have the rabbits cleared from inside the enclosures to save the young trees; rabbits and squirrels between them decimate young trees. This again was Bob's special area of expertise, as was after years in the making of cider, the disposal of wasps nests although it did cost him a very swollen head clearing a nest for John Howe one time. The nest was in some straw bales and John hadn't mentioned to Bob that he'd had a go at it already. Of course as soon as Bob put his head over the stack the wasps were after him. He managed to get the poison in the nest but not before he had been badly stung. *'Sorting the rooks from the jack-daws didn't always come easy.'*

Fences

Farmers you know are make do and menders
When it comes to repairing their gates and their fences
They've got all the gear but don't have the time
So they tie them together with old binder twine.

It is a good fence that can stand a friendly nudge from a half ton bullock and it is little wonder that folk lore pokes fun and that the fence repairs are always getting ahead of the stock man.

The pride of putting up a new wire all tensioned and shiny, stapled three rows down and critically about three foot high is soon lost on a farm labourer because he knows his work is [*not able to resist the pun]* of a stop gap nature.

But in young Bob's case it was never a problem because if a fence could not be by-passed then it could be vaulted, one hand on the post and over he went. However, it must be remembered that young Bob carries the 'young' prefix like the American son might carry the affix 'junior' and that people don't stay juniors or young forever. Bob was small of stature and he was more likely in his later years to duck through the middle and top wires risking a tear in his jacket rather than trying to vault the fence. Of course sometimes on a new section, the wires were so taught even this could cause problems and perhaps on a shoot with other people around it was not a very macho feeling to be ducking through like the ladies.

So, what are we coming to? A farmer, young Bob, out on a shoot with his friends, coming up to a fence, breaks his gun removes the cartridges, everything right so far. Pushes the gun through the fence and decides he will stand on the middle wire and throw his free leg over the top wire and back onto the middle wire again; couldn't be simpler. Now as has already been stated, *ad nausium,* Bob was short of stature, indeed to get somewhat personal, his inside leg measurement was probably less than 29". But let's be fair if the staples hadn't popped on the middle wire all would have been fine, it's happened to most of us, alas pop they did, letting Bob's nine or so stone down not so gently onto the tender region somewhere between his scrotum and his anus.

When Blondini crossed the Niagara Falls on a tight rope he carried a long heavy pole to assist his balance. In Bob's case he wished he weighed less as he teetered on the barbed wire like a cockerel on a washing line, unable to let go, taking as much weight on his hands as possible yelping like a collie pup until two of the shoot arrived to lift him off by the arm pits, laughing outrageously at the possibility that he may be scarred for life in a somewhat, they joshed, redundant part of his anatomy.

The Incident Dressed in Nothing but Fox Skins - 1954

Bob's friend Jesse Millen relates the story that every new years eve Bob could be seen going round the pubs in Tenterden dressed only in Fox skins and carrying a chestnut bat as a club, cave man style, over his shoulder. However his wife Evelyn tells the story of how when Bob's brother Michael served in Kenya during the Mau Mau troubles their platoon came across a deserted terrorist hideout where in one of the huts they found a number of illegal leopard pelts. The order was given that they must be destroyed but Michael could not see the sense in this and quietly pushed one under his tunic to take home. The rest of the operation was quite arduous and in extremely hot conditions and there is no doubt that wearing battle dress *and* a leopard skin was quite a sacrifice. Michael eventually was demobbed and he brought his trophy home for it to be greatly coveted by his elder brother, young Bob who, says Evelyn, wore it and nothing else, *not* during his new years reverie exploits, but on a very special ***St Valentines*** dance at the Tenterden Club when outside there was snow on the ground. He visited every pub in the town then capped it all by taking first prize in the fancy dress contest. 'but' she added, 'the chestnut bat is probably accurate.'

It is extremely puzzling to imagine grown men doing the dressing up bit. Okay, young Bob was an exception and it became expected of him, but he infected those around him in such a way that they did it too. It didn't need to be a special celebration, like New Year or Christmas because if he asked them to dress up as tramps and turn up at a local pub, they entered into the young Bob spirit of mischief and turned up.

There was a time when a bounty was paid on the skins of vermin, Foxes, squirrels and the like, as these pests did, and still do lots of damage to domestic birds and young trees.

There was once a trade in the pelts to be had in Germany and before that the felt trade, but these days had passed on. Even so Bob could not resist keeping the brushes of the foxes killed on his land and one year before the Boxing Day hunt assembled outside the Woolpack Ph.. for their stirrup cup he dressed *[nay, some insist festooned]* the traditional Christmas tree with, of all things, the large number of brushes he'd collected over the year.

Indeed when Bob lived at Goodshill he wired *[the skilful art of setting fox snares]* twenty five foxes in one winter off one hedgerow alone

The Ashford Valley Fox Hounds always used to send Bob a couple of complementary car park and refreshment tickets for their 'Point to Point' meeting but they took umbrage that year saying he'd killed so many foxes he was doing them a disservice and no tickets were forthcoming.

It goes without saying that young Bob had the last laugh as the following year he dressed up a dead fox in pink hunting clothes complete with hat and sat it in the hunt master's car, paws on the steering wheel whilst the master was living it up at the hunt ball at Tenterden town Hall.

Back row. Left to right, Michael Luck. Titch Pearce. Tony Ogden, Peter Miller, Alan Pickford. Front row. left to right, Bob Luck. John Fuggle. John Sims

The Cider Maker
Frogshole 1935 to 1978

There was always more to the making of cider than even the most informed layman could imagine. During the process one of the greatest nuisances was the wasp and more particularly when pressing and sugaring was being done late in the season. The two brothers Bob and Michael used to be paid six pence [2.5new pence] for each nest they found and marked with a stick.

The task fell to everyone to try and keep them down but to none more so than Charlie Hollyer who went round the marked nests after old Bob had poisoned the insects. Charlie's job was to dig out the nest and see to it the grubs were destroyed too as there would very soon be a whole new swarm to contend with if the grubs were missed. Charlie was good at his job remembering where the poisoned nests were and tackling them with a spade.

But there had to be a first time, a time when his memory might just fail him. Of course the inevitable happened. He set about digging out what he thought was an already poisoned nest comfortable in the knowledge that he had only the pupae and grubs to destroy.

The shock of the angry swarm took him by surprise for at first he thought they were a few 'left overs or early fliers' not a whole swarm. Hell no! Soon he was flaying wildly with his arms at the little devils as they clung to his hair and got up his shirt. They stung him wildly again and again until he was forced to bolt full speed back towards the house, and hopefully safety, followed by the evil noisy black cloud of wasps. Charlie pulled off his shirt and flayed the air hoping to disperse them still running towards the farm house. By now some had settled inside the waist band of his slacks and he undid them too. The stinging sensation was numbing and the adrenalin flowed so vigorously through his body he ran with the energy of a youth not caring or thinking of anything but to be rid of the devils free-riding on his body.

Old Bob was in the kitchen looking out of the door when his now demented employee exploded into the yard before him, naked save for his boots, his trousers round his knees and batting his body furiously with his hands.

Bob was dumbstruck at first, and then thinking to protect his wife's embarrassment he called into the back of the house. *'Don't come out here Missus, Charlie Hollyer's naked!'*

But Freda misheard the shout thinking her husband had said. *'Come out here, Charlie Hollyer's fainted!'* and so picked up a damp tea cloth and rushed out into the yard.

Charlie Hollyer figured quite a lot in old Bob's life at Frog's Hole , in as much as he was a retainer, an odd job man, and happy enough to be *'pissed out of his mind'* most of the time. It should not be forgotten that although Charlie was nearly always drunk he was looked after; like the time he complained of a howling tooth ache such that even old Bob and the others could stand it no more. Old Bob proceeded to ply Charlie with rum until he was almost unconscious and then with the aid of the other workers removed the rotten tooth. Cider maker or dentist it made no difference to old Bob and there is little to wonder about where young Bob got his confidence and sense of mischief.

Charlie failed to turn up for work next morning and old Bob began to think he might just have broken the man's jaw extracting the tooth. A search party was being organised when bright as a button Charlie appeared on his bike shouting out. *'Call yourselves bloody dentists. You silly lot of buggers have pulled out the wrong tooth!'*

Special visitors to Frog's Hole were often invited to sample Cider from old Bob's extra ordinary casks. No one knew about these casks, customs and excise especially. Moreover they were more potent that the vintage Cider he was famous for, and flavoured too with such flavours as peppermint and orange, never seen on the market anywhere then or since.

To make things more entertaining he had had made some of what are called *'dribbling glasses'*. The reader may be familiar with the construction of these glasses which had very fine holes just below the bottom lip line cleverly concealed in the design of the glass. Of course what was funny then may not be funny today but old Bob certainly got his kill watching his guests thinking they'd slurped their drink when all the time it was the glass.

Jimmy French relates the story of being offered a glass of the special one day after doing a bit of baling at the farm next door to old Bob's place. Of course old Bob only gave

Old Bob and Charlie Mynard
Taking a glass of cider at Frogs Hole

you 'a glass' unless he was in the mood or you were somebody special your self; or indeed somebody he wanted to get at like the two local bobbies he sent back to their car in a somewhat wobbly state one time.

This particular evening after loading up the bales young Bob and Michael asked Jimmy down into the cellar. Old Bob was away, and they all enjoyed not one but two glasses of special which was fine until the time came to walk. If it hadn't been for Michael I'd have walked straight into the pond relates Jimmy. That wasn't the end to the story for as it was evening Michael wanted some help with getting the turkeys in. The turkey pen was just a fenced off area consisting of brambles and bracken with a turkey house at one end. He told Jimmy to watch the birds and count them as they came through. Jimmy was feeling half cut and it was nearly dark, the turkeys were dark and he looked and looked but couldn't see any.

'How many is that?' Michael shouted.

'No none yet.' Jimmy replied.

Jimmy could hear Michael struggling through the brambles.

'How many now?'

'No still can't see any.' Jimmy answered again.

At this point Michael burst through the undergrowth shouting with a gasp of frustration. *'I'm not surprised you silly old bugger you're sat over the bloody pop-hole.'*

Jimmy had felt so wobbly and light headed that he'd sat down on the ramp that leads up to the pop-hole into the turkey house. No way would any self respecting turkey try and get past with him sat there.

Jimmy French remembers Cecil Page having a similar 'two glass' experience at the hands of young Bob, indeed he left the cellar quite upright to the admiration, no doubt, of any observers there may have been. He did however waken up feeling terribly cold in the morning lying between two rows of his early potato crop.

Charlie Hollyer ran a thin line between full time inebriated employment and the sack. He was often threatened with what old Bob called the ***D.C.M.*** It being wartime the initials seemed appropriate, like a medal or something, but they stood for ***Don't Come Monday***. Indeed he was actually sacked and protested saying *'Does this mean I can go and work anywhere I want?'* When he received the affirmative reply off he went, only to return the next day ready for work. *'What are you doing here?'* It was demanded of him. *'You did say I could work anywhere I wanted and I quite like it here.'* he responded. Considering his employer had removed the wrong tooth some weeks before this was loyalty indeed.

Old Bob Luck used to buy forty gallon used oak Rum barrels. These barrels had once contained Rum and were to be used eventually for laying up the vintage cider for which he was famous. The barrels were tipped up and put out in the sun to dry each positioned over a collecting jar because Bob had discovered that this action resulted in as much as one gallon of *'free'* rum per forty gallon barrel leached out of the wood by the sun's heat. Such rum as was the nearly neat alcohol used to put out [*and he meant out!*] old Bob's dental patient.

Part of the process of cider making is the sugaring. This was done two and half pounds to the gallon with a stainless steel funnel through the bung into each barrel. The sugar they used was Demerara, as white sugar neither imparted the same flavour or the dark golden colour that Demerara did. The sugar was bought in twenty Ton loads *[that's 2,240 lb tons not the tonnes we are becoming used to today.]* Each bag weighed two and a quarter hundredweight, that's 252lbs and had to be carried from the lorry up to the granary. One hundred and seventy seven sacks.

In these days of European laws and measures it is now thought that forty kilogram's [80lbs] is a reasonable maximum for one man to lift. Every time they had a delivery of sugar, nine sacks to each ton had to be off loaded and moved to the granary. This was a massive amount of work for young Bob who weighed in about nine stone [108lbs.] and was therefore lifting well over his own body weight twice over.

Of course he did have some help but most of the carrying fell to him, because his helper, although quite strong was also tall, and at the top of the granary steps the door being in the roof of the building was very low. The tall man could not bend his knees to get through the door with a 2.25cwt sugar sack across the back of his neck without crippling his knees.

As if the job wasn't hard enough, the sugar often hardened in the sack, which after a few carries skinned the shoulders. One time old Bob complained to Tate & Lyle the suppliers and their representative came down for a word. Old Bob let the Rep see the scratches on young Bob's back and the Rep was quite sympathetic but by the time their business was completed and it was time for him to leave Bob was working elsewhere on the farm. The Rep's sympathy however had not diminished so he tipped Bob's helper a fiver in compensation, much to young Bob's disgust when he heard about it as it was he who had the sore back.

Young Bob didn't need fame by association he was popular enough in his own right locally, but there is no doubting there was pleasure to be had in meeting famous clients swapping a few stories or sharing a drink with them. One such acquaintance was the proprietor of Black Boys 14th century coach house, [the village and pub named after the charcoal burners of that era] Ronald Shiner the popular film and music hall performer. Another and perhaps more awe inspiring was the famous survivor of the world heavy weight contest with Rocky Marcianno, the famous, Don Cockel who ran the Jenny Lind public House in Hastings.

It wasn't just drinking establishments but often the large houses of the gentry or the famous. It seemed no delivery was too small or too out of the way. Captain Parry the distinguished naval officer who commanded the HMS Achilles at the battle of the river Plate was on the list.

It is strange that folk lore has pin pointed Somerset as the home of British Cider through such songs as *'Let's go down to Zomerzet where the Zider Apples grow*! Sung by the Wurzles in the fifties. It is true to say that the big names have after all been more enduring, ***Taunton Cider Co.*** in particular. It is however worthy of note that when the West Country dairy farmers Milk tankers delivered milk to Kent from Wincanton. Their tanks were washed out so they could take Bob Luck's apple juice back with them. 100,000 galls went back to Taunton Cider, similarly Merrydown in Sussex, and Hayward & Greengrow in Kent who Bob eventually bought out, and many others were supplied by Bob Luck at the height of his production.

Cider production started with the readiness of the fruit about the end of August with a variety called the Beauty of Bath accompanied by the Derby Apple and followed by the Early Worcesters, this continued through the autumn and into winter when the cold stores emptied other varieties but mainly Bramleys. The Bramley was particularly well suited to Cider making as they gave two and a half gallons of juice to the bushel and were easy to press.

Late cider production had its problems not least of all the low temperatures. Fermentation depends upon the right temperature but long before that process begins the pulp has to be spread on to mats prior to pressing and often the large stainless steel containers were frozen. Spreading the pulp was done by hand onto cloths over wicker mats, covered over and followed by another and another and so on before going under the huge press. Evelyn records how they carried one employee from the Cider sheds stiff with the cold, eyes glazed over and past shivering, into the warm of the house to thaw him out as he had passed out. This certain individual was sent home to recover, hyperthermia, exposure who knew any different? *'The poor old sod was just plain frozen!*

As a break from routine one lunch time one of Bob's mates had brought a cross bow to the works at Frogshole. Bob was itching to have a go with it. Anything that fired a missile was irresistible to Bob and with so many apples about the cider works his vision of William Tell immediately manifested inside his head. Of course there were no volunteers so he aimed at the tree across the yard. His aim for this first time experience was rubbish for the bolt flew like an exocet ripping a pair of Elizabeth Mynard's knickers off the washing line and pinning them inaccessibly to the bough of the oak. There is no record as to how this delicate item was retrieved or explanation for the quiet sniggers when Charlie Mynard restarted after lunch.

A Moment of Distinction - 1971

They say that everyone has a moment of fame, but in the case of young Bob Luck these moments punctuated his life, however the whole family was to share a moment of distinction when on Sunday the 31st October 1971 an Independent Television Co. Sought permission to transmit a programme called 'Farm Progress' It featured Bob Luck & Family from Frogshole Farm Benenden in Kent and also featured was John Bligh of Red House Benenden, his main apple supplier.

The Director was a Mr A Howard and the production assistant was N Wiltshire. In the script the programme participants are named as Mark Jenner, Bob Luck, Michael Luck and John Bligh. The running time was to be twenty four minutes and thirty seconds with no commercial break. The outdoor filming of course had preceded the broadcast and Mr Jenner lead into the transmission with the caption:-

'Examining with farm by farm examples the ways in which British Agriculture is meeting its current problems.'

The film commentary which was read approximately as follows was interspersed by three discussions; *[not documented]*

Vintage & Ordinary Cider. Preparing pulp for animal feed & feeding the animals.

T.V. Commentary:

These lovely Cox's are for eating. But not all the apples in this quality orchard will reach the shops. Some will be rejected because of the size, or blemish; some will be gathered from the ground, and these apples will go to cider making.

The owner of Red House fruit farm at Benenden is John Bligh. He has sixty acres of Cox and plums- about ninety percent of the farm is in Cox, with Worcester pollinators.

There is then a digression as the film pans around Red House and its 15th century attributes and grounds

John Bligh has picked up to 1000 bushels to the acre this year, although the average would be 6-700, the great bulk of it grade one fruit.

It is a frost free site which his father had from 1918, Mr Bligh took it over in 1952. About 95% of his fruit makes grade one. But some must fail, and he is fortunate in having an outlet for rejects and drops at a cider factory in the same village. Loads of apples from the ground or from the grader can go straight from his farm to the factory by lorry.

In the pack house the grader will account for most of the cider rejects. John Bligh sends for cider making between three and four thousand bushels of apples per season. He's paid £10 a ton worth about £600.

A regular part time team is employed in grading and packing 30lb boxes. John Bligh's contribution to the cider factory -50-60 tons –is only a small proportion of the total reject fruit required by this outlet, about 500 tons in a season. The supply is supplemented by other growers in the area.

Size grading is restricted to 55mm and 50mm, the larger size going away to Spitalfields in London. Marketing is through a commercial company supplied by 6-8 growers; Although not under contract.

The smaller fruit will be held until Christmas in cold stores of 10,000 bushels Capacity.

It is a clever pack- whatever the size of apple, when filled it will weigh approximately 30lbs, with at most a 3lb margin which can be easily corrected. Of course there's no expensive handling or packaging where apples for cider making are concerned.

Their juice will end up in a barrel like this one – and this is Mr Bob Luck of Frogshole Farm, the cider maker stacking an empty. Bob Luck is a farmer too, with 250 acres, beef cattle and sheep.

All traditional enterprises – none more so than cider – and the Luck family at Benenden make 70,000 gallons of it a year, stored in barrels.

Mr Luck started in 1935, with a small hand press on an 18 acre farm. It was a bad first year, apples for cider making

were in short supply and local farmers who customarily bought –in, or made, 30-120 gallons of cider couldn't restock. Mr Luck managed to acquire some apple juice at this time and that's how the business began.

His cider helped supplement the wartime beer ration and in 1945 he installed heavy plant and hydraulic presses.

In the press room apples of all varieties and type drawn from local growers are elevated up to a mill for pulping. As pulping continues the press is gradually built up in a series of wooden frames called mats – about fifteen in all.

The pulp won't be wasted. After pressing, it will be carted later to the fattening of cattle and sheep on Mr Luck's farm. The Luck's reckon you can fatten a bullock on apple pulp.

There's not much juice from pulping. What there is flows with the rest, into a holding pit for 300 gallons later to be pumped into barrels.

When there are enough mats containing the pulp, they are moved across to the big 100 ton hydraulic presses that exert a pressure of half a ton per square inch and this is where the apple juice really flows.

There are two Luck brothers. The elder, Bob Luck junior, is in charge of the press room and his wife Evelyn works with him. They also tend and feed the stock.

The 120 gallon wooden casks are the main means of storing Bob Luck's cider, and the juice flowing from the presses is pumped straight to them via the holding pit.

From them, after further processing, will come ordinary cider, at 7-8% proof, and the apple wine of Kent better known as vintage cider, at 22-23% proof.

These are vintage cider barrels. White sugar is 'fed' to the cider to promote fermentation and it may stay in cask two to three years. It's pretty potent.

The term 'vintage' in this case has nothing to do with the year or one particular harvest.

Out of cask, the cider must be purified by various methods and here Michael Luck, the younger brother, is in charge. He uses centrifuges to dissipate any solids in the cider – for example any specks of pulp which might have got through.

The cider is then passed through two separate filters. In

one of them a special powder is introduced which coats the filter plates and improves filtration.

The liquid which finally goes into cask or jar, whether ordinary or vintage cider, will be bright and clear. It is sold in the cask, in gallon or half gallon jars and it costs 10 new pence a pint for ordinary and 12 new pence, a Pony glass for vintage cider – the wine of Kent.

It is largely local retailing, through the pubs, off-licenses and cider bars, roughly travelling over a 30 mile radius from Frogshole Farm which includes the big coastal towns.

The transmission ends with the usual thanks to their hosts and the toast 'here's Luck.'

No doubt old Bob thought the programme good for business or he would never have entertained it, he could, there was no doubt, have put more zing into the narrative with some of his catch phrases; *'There's a baby in every bottle' 'Air raid tonic' 'Love potion'* and many others. He may even have changed the back ground music to his preferred Acker Bilk who himself had enjoyed more than one glass at the Hasting Carnival in Sussex the year before.

Of Course, this pleasing twenty minute television programme with its warm sunny soft spoken narrator, its highly skilled camera crew panning around Frog's Hole belies the reality of Cider making. Like many country programmes, the *'down your way'* balmy day image with its canned *'birds song, running stream, insect buzzing'* sound tracks bear little resemblance to the rigours that often accompanied the work.

The Cider maker's day began at 7.30 am and finished at 5pm or was supposed to, but you can't stop in the middle of a process and you weren't finished until you'd cleaned up; making Cider is a messy business.

The apples came in all sorts of containers, not just in clean neat 40lb bushel boxes like in the film. They came in 'sacks' 'bulk bins', 'tipper trailers' and lorries, and were tipped at the foot of an elevator which carried them up into the mill. In the mill they were chopped up mechanically into pulp. Because of the acidity of the fruit all the metal coming into contact with it was stainless steel. The mill held 37 bushels of pulped apples [37x40lbs=1480 lbs] measured automatically. Below the mill was a track supporting a stainless steel tray about 6" deep by 2'6" square. In the tray was laid a semi rigid matt made of woven osier willow and on top of this was placed a wooden frame and over that laid diagonally was a square nylon sheet

The pulp could be released to fall from the mill above in measured quantities. Two operatives standing either side of the frame would spread the pulp with their hands and then fold the corners of the nylon sheet into the middle before adding yet another tray. The act of folding the cloths in this way was called making *'a cheese'*. This process was repeated until the progressive number of trays had reached the right height to fit under the press.

At this stage the operative's arms are cold, wet and sticky to the elbows.

The three hydraulic presses were electric made by H Beare & Sons of Newton Abbot. Their capacity was one and a half tons to the square inch. All the presses had a linked drainage system of pipes to a 300 gallon underground collection chamber. Some varieties of apples were better than others, the worst being over ripe Cox's and Worcesters because they were soft and not very juicy, their pulp was very slippery which made pressing slow and difficult.

If rushed the cheeses didn't hold up and had to be rebuilt.

Although rubber boots and aprons were worn, when a bulge in one of the cheeses appeared there was little warning before, under such pressure, a huge jet of ice cold apple juice would drench the operator. As Evelyn relates her hair had to be washed every evening and her trouser stood up on their own, amusing though it may seem it must be remembered that the apple juice wasn't warm and in the winter often only a degree or two above freezing.

The Mill held 37 bushels of pulped apples, in theory measured precisely, however if the apples were larger than usual then the elevator fed them into the pulp mill faster than the pressings could be built up. So here we have a Charlie Chaplin Modern Times scenario where automation goes berserk.

'The elevator is lifting the fruit and the fruit is being pulped and delivered at such a rate that the operatives can't keep up.' Well not exactly. One burst cheese, and the Mill must be stopped by tripping the elevator circuit as the Mill continues all the while it is being fed by the elevator. The operatives can tell if the Mill is full by the sound of the knives in the Mill, but if the Mill was very full, stopping the elevator did not 'immediately' stop the Mill delivering, especially if the apples were large, so the operatives continued to be supplied with sticky cold apple pulp dripping down on them from the overflowing Mill.

Having drained all the juice the trays then had to have the pulp *[sometimes referred to as mash or pomace]* removed. This now has the appearance of cardboard both in colour and consistency and in some cases stubbornness as the Cox's left sticky lumps clinging to the cloths. The pulp was used as cattle feed and they seemed to fatten well on it. As young Bob said, the ITV film didn't show them skidding about in their wellies, soaked to the skin and frozen to the bone. It didn't show the wasps and the annoying legions of fruit flies or the back breaking loading and lifting that went with the production, it didn't even say that after all, such a fine product's reputation wasn't earned without hard work.

Outside the mill were rows of barrels bought it from such firms as Allan, Skinner & Parr of London and Ellis Son & Vidler of Hastings. They had been used before for Wine, Rum or even Whisky. The sizes varied 140, 120, 60 and 48 gallons being usual. They were filled under pressure not always without mishap as it was not unknown for the pressure to blow the head out of the barrel instead of coming back through the bung.

Fermentation of course begins after filling. To this day some producers rely on the natural sugars and yeasts on the actual apples to trigger fermentation for rough cider. In old Bob's case the quality was important to him and whereas he produced many varieties, his vintage cider, so called, was consistently good, being between 22 and 23 percent proof after four years in the barrel. This product attracted the customs and excise officers regularly to take samples and to set the appropriate duty. It was not of course just the appeal of the alcohol content but the rich colour given it by the Demerara sugar and the mellow smoothness that categorised it as 'vintage' not in the sense of old wine but in the sense of fine quality.

Other less meritorious ciders were produced some even sweetened with saccharin, as the market demanded all grades. Two gallon stone jars complete with screw cap and

Old Bob and the elevator at Frogs Hole farm Cider Works

tap and the words Bob Luck Cider were the best sellers and are still seen today in antique shops around the south east. One gallon, glass demi-johns, one and two litre bottles catered for all demands. Alas, the demise of the Bob Luck cider industry preceded the introduction of cans, currently the most efficient way of selling small amounts in large quantities, a system that would no doubt have appealed to old Bob's business sense.

Old Bob's business sense carried as always an air of humour. His Lorries carried the greeting on the front 'Here's Luck' and on the tail board 'Cheerio!' initially, later versions added the words 'and Bob's your Uncle!'

A Day's Outing

Like many men Bob hated shopping and rarely went up to town, [London, the smoke, call it what you like.] but perhaps due to some mental aberration forgetting for a moment just how much London department stores differ from the soft countryside of Millpond Farm, he told Evelyn she had a treat in store; Christmas shopping in London.

Warren's Coaches, as they still do to day, ran outings up to London. The pick-up point was the Crown Ph. at St Michaels. Not having done this before they between them reckoned a straight run up to the City would take little over the hour.

Of course they had not bargained for the grand tour of out lying villages, stopping at Pubs and post offices on the way to collect others of like mind. The journey took nearly three hours. It was the fourth of December 1989 and a freezing wind was theirs for company as, along with the rest of the coach load, they were dropped off at Hyde Park Corner.

Country people, especially farmers, don't like wasting time. They rise early and get on with their day's work and here they were with half the day gone and nothing achieved.

Of course as people who do this regularly at this time of year would expect Harrods and for that matter any other major departmental store to be crowded; it was here amongst the jostling shoppers that Bob's dislike for the whole business began to resurface.

Soon he began to feel the same in reverse as a city gent complete with bowler and brolly would if deposited in a hop garden in Kent at the middle of winter. No way could he endure this any further so, taking Evelyn's arm he made his excuses, pointing out a Pub on the corner opposite the store, saying *'Come and find me when you're done, that's where I'll be.'*

Evelyn didn't buy too much, okay she didn't need Bob's

approval but to have had him there at her side might have liberated that feeling of 'what do you think? Shall we shan't we?' spirit of spending. Before heading for the coach Bob took her off to an Indian restaurant for a late lunch, glad to be away from the mêlée of the Christmas crowd.

Pick up time was about four thirty, the coach was late, and an Indian lunch and a few drinks only seem to keep you warm for so long. The shoppers with their carrier bags and packages were left stamping their feet to keep warm in the stiff breeze. It wasn't long before Bob was caught up in conversation with a young woman, all top coat and legs, who as Evelyn was standing apart, clearly thought he was unattached.

The cold seemed not to affect her as after some considerable discourse she left and Evelyn now curious to know what it was all about asked. *'What was all that about then?'*

'I've just been invited to a party.' Bob replied with a grin, then added. *'And you know what sort of party, don't you?'*

As Evelyn relates later 'It was some old Tom looking for business.'

That day out *'The treat'* hadn't ended there, because it snowed on the way home and the coach which had no heating stopped at Frant, Ticehurst, Wadhurst and every other village you can think of on the way back to Tenterden finally dropping them off on the Biddenden road which left them with a good mile and a half to walk laden down with shopping bags, and not in the best of humour. Fortunately, as ***'luck'*** would have it, you might say, along came their daughter Julie quite by chance to give them a lift home. Bob however swore it would be the last time.

Of course there's no road as long as a cold road or a dark road for that matter and Norton's lane which runs from the Biddenden road past Children's farm down to the end of the concrete road and their home at Millpond Farm would have been a very uncomfortable mile in the snow.

That same mile of road can be quite pleasant in the summer and one day Bob found himself looking over the fence of Merv's allotment at the family gathering of his friend Jim Thompson. It was a nice day and they had decided to have a picnic there. They greeted Bob as his head and shoulders appeared over the hawthorn hedge. After the usual cheeky pleasantries Bob said.

'Yer couldn't give us a lift down ter my place could yer Jim?'

Jim looked up at Bob thinking how very hot it was and how it would only take a minute or two to run his old mate home. '*Yeah alright Bob,*' he said. And with that he scooped up his grandson Sean and put him in the seat behind them in the car.

They shot down the lane crossed the junction, sped along the concrete road, and before you knew it there they were sat in the yard at Millpond farm. '*It's good of you to give us a lift Jim I know its not far and all that but since my hip operation it sometimes plays me up.*

'*Oh*' said Jim, laughing. '*Trouble with you Bob you had too many knee tremblers in your youth it's them wot's knackered yer hip hey?'*

They both laughed, then in the pause that followed, Bob replied. '*You must be a f***ing cripple then ha ha!*'

When Jim got back to his family picnic seated comfortably in the shade, tea and sandwiches and all the civilized niceties of the summers day. Who should relate word for word for the whole families ears the conversation he had just heard, between Bob and his Grandfather, but Jim's grandson Sean.

Of course there were other outings in their lives mainly involving Bob; his flights across the channel for duty free beer and tobacco outdone only by the booze cruises on Seacat or one of the other cross channel operators.

Evelyn rarely went with them because she was a poor sailor but on one occasion when she did she was so queasy that she sought out the only place she could stand it. Like many poor sailors she had probably been told not to take her eyes off the horizon, the theory being that is the only thing not moving. Fixed in this position, semi comfortably with her back against the superstructure, no one could find her, she certainly wasn't moving. Bob whose only thought had been the duty free was now distraught having searched the ship twice over looking for her.

'Where've yer been Evelyn? I've bloody near walked to

France and back looking for you. I thought you might have gorn over the side'

Then there was the infamous twenty pound note trip. This involved an outing to buy beer and baccy from a newsagent in Belgium. The trip was organised by Ernie Wren the landlord of the Vine Ph.., they took Larky Harris and his missus Paula, Bill Relf and Gordon Lilly. In the shop they paid for their goods with a twenty pound note a lot of money in those days. The note had been placed on the counter with some newspapers. They were just about to leave when the proprietor asked for the money and of course they said, we paid you. First of all the whole troop of them searched the shop and papers fold by fold but the note could not be found. By now the rather untrusting proprietor had called the gendarmes who listened willingly to their countryman and were ready to cart the whole English party off to the gendarmerie. Soon things had become rather serious and but for fluent interpretation by Gordon Lilly they felt they may all have been locked up. As it was they had to go home without their precious beer that time.

Bonfire Nights

Any occasion where country people gathered together for a night out attracted young Bob. Like many young men he liked a bit of fun and Bonfire night was no exception.

Headcorn in ***1950*** was the scene of one such night out and the village bonfire was in every body's opinion quite a *'good un'*. So good in fact that always there were a few Bobbies or specials on duty. Bob and his friends Wally Maskell and Ray Millen were with a group of merrymakers threading their way through the crowd that night when the local police sergeant, full of his own importance, and complete with loud speaker van decided that they should be reminded about the dangers of throwing fireworks.

'Ladies and gentlemen' the loud hailer hissed and crackled. *Please be aware of the dangers..'* Bob had had enough of this; the announcement after all was worse than British Railways and harder to understand. Weren't they here to have a good time and let off a few bangers? Bob's sense of fun and justice railed against this big brother intrusion.

Inside his pocket he carried a rope cartridge he'd brought with him from Goodshill farm. Now a rope cartridge consists of a string of cartridges connected in series on a rope. This acts as a fuse which burns down at a given rate to explode repeatedly in cherry orchards to scare off pigeons and the like. Bob had cut out the cartridges to use as bangers and promptly fished one out of his pocket and lit it.

As the fuse burned down the question was where to throw it. It must have seemed obvious to Bob for in a rush of blood he threw it at the police van; didn't that after all represent the authority he railed against? His aim was better or worse than anyone could have hoped, depending on one's view, for by dint of ill fortune it ricocheted off his intended target and went straight down the horn of the loud speaker cutting short the next announcement of '*ladies and gent..*' with a loud '*bang!*' nearly breaking the now emerging and bewildered announcer's jaw in the process.

Now followed a rather serious '*who threw that?*' inquisition in which an individual pointed the finger at Bob; it looked for some worrying moments that he might be arrested.

It is testament to Bob's popularity that at this crucial moment of arrest there were enough of his friends in the crowd to say '*No, no, it was someone over there. It wasn't him.*' The policeman, then turned on the original finger pointer, telling him off for not being sure of his facts, whilst Bob kept quiet relieved to have got away with it and no doubt feeling just a little guilty.

Battle

Another Town that was popular amongst young people at bonfire time was Battle where the George Hotel always held a Bonfire night dance. The dance going on upstairs and the fire burning out in the grounds nearby was always very popular.

It was about the year ***1954*** when the man made bacteria Myxomatosis was decimating the rabbit population in this part of Kent.

The link between this bacteria and bonfire night in Battle was made significant by the fact that no one wanted rabbits even although the ministry said the flesh was unaffected by the disease; no one would touch them. So therefore, like some stock market commodity the Ferret *[the poacher's friend]* had suddenly become redundant.

Upstairs in the George that night if the couples weren't quickstepping around the floor to 'Put another nickel in the nickelodeon,' then they were mooning to the strains of 'Irene Goodnight.' *[Mooning in an old fashioned sense that is.]* As the beer had flowed generously on a late licence and the band thumped gently on into the morning, nothing had ever been so serene as the crowd shuffled around the dance floor.

Young Bob had other ideas, as from his pocket, in the dim glow of the rotating constellation sending little spots of light moving round the hall, he took out the pink eyed Ferret which he'd decided was about to go back into employment.

The Ferret was loosed off into the moving forest of silk stockinged ankles, turn-ups and crepe soles, with a length of string and squib attached. The bang was ear splitting, but the animal was less frightened than half the females in attendance and caused a screaming mayhem before disappearing somewhere behind the lead guitarist.

The ferret was never seen again or it would have earned a bonus from Bob, but there's no doubt it cleared the floor of the George that night alright.

Rye: The Railway Hotel

The Railway Hotel at Rye was popular too. On bonfire night even Londoners descended on the town to join in the reverie. Bob and a pal or two were in the Railway Hotel having a few pints before going off to look at the fire. Inside the public bar a rather well made up lady, tarty Bob would have said, sat at the old iron framed upright piano knocking out popular songs much to the appreciation of the lads and customers alike.

It had been raining outside and it was about this time the advent of the plastic pixie hood was catching on. Our lady pianist was no exception for hers worn neatly over her permanent wave to make sure it remained so was now pushed nonchalantly back. As everyone got merrier so to Bob the pixie hood seemed to take on the mantle of challenge, after all every time it was his round didn't he have to squeeze past, What if they dropped a little beer in the hood each time, how much would it hold? A pint, two?

So the evening wore on and the lads filled it up drop by drop. Choruses of 'London Town' and 'My old man' tinkled into the night and at last she gave it a rest put down the lid, lit herself a fag and got up to go. Saying her cheerio's she stopped at the door and pulled over her hood.

Bob and his friends would have, in a more reasonable state, been apologetic, but as pranks go it was a success for not only did the lady drench her hair, extinguish her fag and ruïn her make-up in one go, but Bob and his country pals learned exactly what colour real London language can be like and were quick to side step the slaps and flaying arms thrown in their direction.

Still at Rye, same occasion, but another year and this time Bob and his mates had been doing the rounds to finish up at the famous Mermaid Hotel. The hotel had as good a reputation then as it has to day for good food and perhaps a better class of clientele. Inside there had been what Northerners might call *'a bit of a do'*. It was a special evening to celebrate Bonfire night. The mayor was there in all his finery, chain of office and red faced. His councillors and a good many others standing side by side like so many penguins with their beers; and the ladies with their gin's chatting the evening away in good spirits.

Whether the thought of the stink bomb was premeditated or not it is hard to know as on this and other occasions it seems Bob was always prepared for mischief. To night was no exception. There is no doubt Bob never felt inferior, country people were the best, there was no doubt about that, best suits or no best suits. They muscled their way to the bar and ordered up a round, and as they tipped up the bottoms of their glasses perhaps they decided the company too stuffy, but whatever signed their death warrant it was done, for in an instant young Bob had crushed the stink bomb under his heel, the phosphorous met the oxygen and ignited the sulphur and he and his mates left.

Out side Bob and his mates stood across the road to watch.

The appalling stench of the bomb, these things smoulder slowly, pervading slowly at first, creeping like the dry ice on the Palladium stage, through the public bar and then, the hall, then the saloon. People coughed and moved sideways, put down their drinks and made for the doors. Soon the smell of rotten eggs was so overpowering they pushed and shoved to escape. The sash window at the front went up and out came a leg followed by the rest of a young man followed by another still holding their pint glasses.

There was it seems no escape from Bob at bonfire night.

Old Bob purchased two hundred acres of Heronden from Evelyn's Grandfather Tom Clarke about ***1959*** much to the delight of Young Bob who along with Evelyn spent a lot of time there on the levels feeding the mallard for shooting. The birds could be encouraged when the levels were under a few inches of water by scattering barley into the slops as this seasonal flooding was called.

Bob's father decided that the old track running along the

edge of Gazedown Wood and long over grown should be cleared, as it would make a better access to the levels than the rather steep Foxbury Bank. This clearance meant burning all the scrub as a result. It was during this clearance Bob discovered a world war two incendiary bomb. It seems that during the war large numbers of these bombs were ditched by the Germans and some definitely aimed at the railway which passes between Gazedown Woods and the Newmill Channel then on its way to Robertsbridge; whatever their intentions this one out of the stick, stuck nose first in a tree in Gazedown Woods.

Bob knew instinctively what it was, undeterred he pulled it from the tree, examined it, shook it and held to his ear before deciding it was safe. It was after all an incendiary bomb and what was a bonfire after all. No reason why it shouldn't become a bombfire was there? So the bomb was cast into the fire without more ado and seemed to make little effect even though the scrub was piled onto it all day.

Some time later on he was having a drink in the local with Evelyn's father, when he slammed down his glass and said. *'Come on Leo let's go and find that bomb.'*

They piled in to the old Ford Popular Bob had at that time, drove out of town down through Morghew, past The Quarter and bumped their way along the newly cleared but no less bumpy track down the side of GazedownWoods.

After scrabbling about in the ashes Bob retrieved the bomb, piled back into the car and bumped their way back as far as Tenterden police station.

Bombs are supposed by design to be very volatile things, often becoming more unstable with age. This bomb had been shaken and subjected to high temperatures and now carted off along a bumpy old track to be unceremoniously dumped on the counter at Tenterden police station in front of a rather surprised if not a little nervous police constable.

But Bob hadn't finished, he had a mind to have this thing as a trophy and told the constable. *'If it's not claimed in three months, it's mine, right?'*

'Wrong! Said a voice from further inside, followed by the appearance of the police sergeant, adding. *'We don't give those things back.'*

You're Barred

Tenterden had until the early nineties a pub called the Cellars, a very popular establishment because it was actually a cellar. A cellar with a barrel bar, low oak beams festooned with the calling cards and foreign bank notes of every nationality. There were other peculiarities hanging in the roof [some unmentionable] along with the tankards of regular drinkers, and all covered with cobwebs.

It is true to say it was not a ladies pub, not downstairs anyway, although the laddish girls of today would have loved it. It was a tied pub run by Fremlin's the Brewers and was very popular.

Ye Olde Cellars
Left to Right: Don Best, John Holdstock, Bob Bell, Louis Pugh, Bill Friend and Leo Bignell

Young Bob frequented the cellars in its turn, so to speak, for all pubs were alright to Bob. But he had for some time been having a running joke with a fellow drinker called Bill who Bob obviously found just a little naïve. Bob had expanded upon the story of Frittenden Brickworks known locally as Frittenden treacle mines. Long since defunct it had always kept this colloquial title so this fact lent a modicum of authenticity to his story should this chap Bill have ever doubted what he was told. Bob spun him the yarn about how the treacle was dug out of the mines with special shovels which had to be heated on braziers so the treacle when cut out in slabs would slide nicely off and into the workers barrows. Bill was nicely set up and ready to accompany Bob to Frittenden when someone felt sorry for the victim to be, and spoilt the fun.

So Bill, Bob's victim was naïve, but you can never be sure about this state, this lack of awareness sometimes present in us all. Bob himself was naïve enough, for without a miss whenever the Salvation Army Officer Percy Hatcher came round the pub, whatever pub he was in, Bob always bought the 'war cry' and always followed it with the question *'Do you save wicked women?'*

'Er Ye..es?' Was always the reply.

'Then save me one for next weekend.' Bob would say.

Bob was drinking in the cellars the evening he should have been challenging the Woodchurch yard of ale champion. His self appointed manager found him there, already on his second pint.

'What yer doin ere? We're supposed ter be over at Woodchurch.' He demanded.

'That's alright a little bit of lubrication won't change nuthin.' Bob replied, and of they went to the Stonebridge Ph. Woodchurch where he beat the local champion Chris Lacki.

One summer's evening Bob and his mates had come back from a days fishing in the channel and were bent on quenching their thirst. They were still in their fishing gear, scruffy, and probably just a little smelly, but then the surroundings weren't all that salubrious, one would never associate the Cellars with the word posh. After waiting quite a while his mates began to get a little impatient to want to go to another pub. Bob was small and the bar staff could probably only see the top of his head. It was then that Bob started to scratch vigorously first his head then his body. Once he'd attracted the attention of the customer next to him he commented loudly. *'Them there old sea lice don't arf get under the skin, whoar!'* One by one the pub's clients edged away, some left and went upstairs. At last the bar was clear and Bob was able to get their drinks in, with a beam of success he ordered, not reckoning he'd been rumbled by the Landlord Dan Field who gave him his order with the firm admonishment. *'Do that again in here young Luck and you're barred!'*

One of the most convenient pubs for young Bob was the William Caxton once known as the Black Horse. It is located at the south end of the high street and impossible to miss when travelling between Heronden from the Small Hythe road and towards Goodshill on the Cranbrook road. Bob had a regular supply of pea silage to take to Goodshill and for those who don't know, silage has a very strong smell. Pea silage is the strongest *[high protein fodder]* and to some is the most obnoxious. Bob used to shift this stuff every Saturday and couldn't resist stopping at the William Caxton for a few pints before continuing on to Goodshill. The smell became too much for the pub's clientele and the barman and Bob fell out over whether it was reasonable to wander into the pub in his mucky clothes reeking of silage and so he was effectively barred from entering the premises on a Saturday. Bob was just a little miffed about this and the next time he was passing, not a Saturday and not in his smelly outfit, but nevertheless with his wellies stuffed full of silage, He ordered a drink , quietly finished it, then with the barman's back turned pulled out the silage and threw it on the fire before leaving. Peter Huckstep relates that the ensuing clouds of hissing stinking white smoke cleared the bar.

The Chinese restaurant in Tenterden used to be a pub called 'This Ancient Borough' but strangely everyone who drank regularly in the town knew it as the 'New Inn'. Young Bob was in there one night drinking with his mate Wally

Maskell who used to roll his own fags and the story goes that whilst Wally was away to the loo Bob doctored his tobacco with Cayenne pepper. When Wally returned and settled down to have a smoke it wasn't long before he was sneezing and coughing and his eyes watering. Wally knew Bob well enough to guess it was Bob and would get his own back later but the barman wasn't amused.

Jim Thompson went to work for old Bob on 1952 helping with what they called the cider run, delivering Bob Luck's cider to old Bob's clients in Kent and Sussex. He recalls on how he and young Bob used to meet fairly regularly in the Crown Ph. in St Michaels for a few pints after the days work. One evening the landlord asked Bob if he could have a barrel of Cider to sell over the bar, well of course there was no reason for not having ordered from the Cider works as Frogs Hole was referred to, so the 'between the lines' inference was obvious, at least to young Bob and the landlord it was. Bob looked at Jim and said. '*You got that motor byke o'yorn out side?*'

Jim had of course, and he agreed to go off to Frogs Hole with Bob on the pillion. They arrived there in the gloom of the evening and between them managed to extract a six gallon barrel from the rest and balance it precariously between them on the motorbike. Back at the Crown Bob was duly paid for the cider and offered Jim some of the money which he declined not because he didn't feel entitled but because he'd observed in the short time he'd known Bob that he never seemed to have much cash on him. Jim was quite happy to have done this as a favour and as he, rightly or wrongly, always thought old Bob and Young Bob synonymous with Bob Luck's cider never thinking there might be anything untoward. So it was a few weeks afterwards that the landlord proposed a repeat order, this time offering them a vehicle and a driver. When they arrived at Frogs Hole they had hardly got out of the vehicle when Jim noticed someone standing in the shadows. '*There's a man standing over there.*' Jim said without lowering his voice. '*What? Let's get going.*' Bob whispered, and they all fled back the way they had come.

For Jim it was this sudden exodus which raised a query in his mind about the validity of the business, until then he had thought nothing of it, after all Bob Luck was Bob Luck to him. Alas that innocence was demolished the next time he went to call at Frogs Hole to collect young Bob, for out came old Bob to growl angrily. *'I think you've got a bloody cheek coming out here after what you've been doing aintcha?'*

Unknown to Jim the Police had been called in to investigate the prowlers and the theft of cider. They had spoken to young Bob and he had made a statement involving Jim. This spoilt his relationship with old Bob who he had got on so well with up until that time. He felt he had betrayed old Bob's trust however unwittingly but it was not to affect his friendship with young Bob.

The cider run at Christmas time carried with it a certain extra as each client would press upon them another drink or something to eat in view of the festive season, indeed Jim relates, it was called the turkey run as always they came home with at least a turkey and on one occasion two. One year Jim was surprised they made it back, having dropped orders off around Sussex all day having the odd pint at every stop. When Jim got off at St Michaels his cheap turkey under his arm and a nice warm feeling somewhere behind his eyes, he watched the lorry edge its way down the lane scraping along the hedge as though feeling for the direction. When he saw Bob next day he asked, *'Did you get home alright Bob?'*

Bob grinned and without hesitation replied. *'The lorry was in the yard this morning when I woke up Thompson.'*

Twenty One Years - 1951

Young Bob's twenty first birthday wasn't quite what he really expected of it. He should, you might expect, have got used to the idea that August is harvest time and one of the busiest times of the year for a young farmer. And so was the year 1951 his twenty first year. He spent all day from early in the morning with the harvesting at the farm and on his way home to Goodshill called in at the Black Horse public House [Now the William Caxton]

Harvesting is a dusty business and perhaps the only other trade of the time that might appreciate the need for a few pints of ale would be the miners. A dry pit that produces *'pneumoconiosis'* by virtue of the coal dust environment in the pits is strangely akin to the disease called *'farmers lung'* in agriculture. Miners would swear that a few pints of ale at least washed down what dust hadn't yet got as far as the lungs.

So here was young Bob dry as a Wyandotte's perch with all the reasons for having a good drink. He was twenty one and just a few people in the bar to share his birthday.

The evening wore on and eventually the time came for him to wend his way back to Goodshill, not worse for drink, but heady with it. Just short of home he noticed over the hedge was a scout camp. The tents were all neatly lined up in rows and the flag hung limp in the warm August air. From the tents came the occasional voices of sleep, a snore, a shout, from lads who were away from home and had had an exciting day. Set apart from the rest was a tent he guessed was the scout master's.

It wasn't dark, the moon was in its second quarter and the countryside had retained some of the glow given by a clear sky.

What if? What if he let down the guy ropes? That would be a birthday treat, but, he pondered, that would take too long, for whilst he was untying one he might be heard, no, he would cut them. There on the block near where they had been cutting firewood was a small chopper. With the stealth of an Indian he moved from tent to tent collapsing them onto the sleeping scouts, finishing off with the scout master's and finally the flag pole. The adrenalin flowed, fought the alcohol in his veins and won, manifesting itself in flight, over the fields to home, silent as a brave, he thought, until he came up against the geese in the yard.

No one can be that quiet, remember, geese saved Rome. Soon he was tucked up in bed sleeping off the adventure and the drink. In the morning things were different.

Whether Bob got a sore head from his night before we shan't know but his conscience was sore. One of his own expressions *was 'An unruly character can only be taken out twice, the second time to apologise.'* He made up his mind to go and apologise to the scout master and scouts. The Scout master he found was quite reasonable about it and even consoled Bob into believing some good had come from it even if only to teach the boys the art of splicing ropes; however he added, the apology although accepted was too late for he had informed the police hours before.

The police acting on the information the scout master had given them, namely, that he had heard the corn rattling followed by the geese alarm calls, brought them to the door at Goodshill where they found the hatchet belonging to the scouts.

Bob was duly summoned before the bench. The magistrate at the time was Stanley Day assisted on the bench by Edith Adams a governor at Homewood school which had opened in 1948.

Mr Day dealt with the matter of unlawful damage and Bob was bound over to behave, due consideration being given to his apologies and the fact that after all it was his birthday. Edith Adams however had other ideas and made sure the court heard a swingeing admonishment about how this behaviour was not to be tolerated. It did not go unnoticed though that Stanley Day gave the matter less importance as friends said he was seen grinning at Bob from the bench.

Although Bob loved Goodshill Farm there were some

painful associations there. Three years before the scouting incident about the beginning of September with the hop drying in full swing he was sat in the Oast when he got a message he was wanted at the house. His mother employed a woman who, for the purpose of discretion we shall call Mrs L, to help with the household chores and it was his mother and Mrs L who confronted him in the kitchen when he went in.

'You've being seeing to my daughter ain't cha?' said Mrs L, stepping forward indignantly. She had a powerful presence and was red faced with anger. Bob's conscience made forming a lie difficult. He had seen much more of Mrs L's daughter than Mrs L was ever going to hear about from him. Before he could utter a word the now angrier lady added. *'You've been givin her one aint cha? You dirty rascal.'* Bob thought to deny it and the denial must have shown on his face for he spoke not a syllable. *'Yes you ave, I know you ave!'* She shouted following her words with a hefty swipe across young Bob's face.

Bob was nonplussed, alone he could have coped, but in front of his mother the embarrassment was severe. His pride hurt and his face stinging he turned and fled to the warmth of the Oast house where Potter Blackford one of his dad's employees was sitting next to the furnace.

'Huh, you look as though you're in a bit of bother Bob.' He said with a grin. Bob related the story admitting he and Mrs L's daughter had *'had it away'* more than once.

Potter laughed, lifted his eyes to bring the teenager a little closer as though to impart one of life's great secrets and in a confidential tone said. *'You should have had the mother first, she's jealous not angry, then borrowed five shilling from the father, and after that taken the daughter; you could really say you'd had all the family then!'*

It was at Goodshill farm they had trouble with the TV reception and to counter this deficiency they erected a substantial forty foot aerial. One night this blew down in a gale and next morning Bob went out to look. What he hadn't noticed was it was lying on the 11,000 volts High Voltage conductor and when he touched it he was knocked off his feet by the shock. They said if he'd not had his wellies on that morning he'd have been a *gonner*. As it was he got his leg pulled unmercifully about how his hair seemed to stand on end for months after.

Goodshill farm was handy for the town and one evening the bar at the Black Horse had been given a bit of a hammering by Bob and Roy Glazier who worked for old Bob. It was Roy who took Bob home that night and guided him quietly into the kitchen to lay him down on the floor next to the Aga to sleep it off. Young Bob woke up about five thirty, feeling stiff and sore, his head thumping and wanting more than anything else to collapse into his own bed. It was about quarter to six he met his father coming down the stair case.

'Where the hell do you think you're going?' old Bob demanded.

'To bed.' Replied young Bob rather pathetically.

'Oh no you're not; you get out and milk those cows, that's where you're going young fella.'

So he was dispatched to do the milking, which after all was his job. Bob however always had a trick or two up his

Young Bob could sleep on the back of a cow and the idea may not have been his owm.

sleeve and one quite unique accomplishment often saved the day when it came to the subject of sleep. Bob could sleep on the back of a cow. Evelyn relates that unless witnessed by 'yer very own eyes' it is hard to believe it possible.

For a man with a hangover and desperate to get his head down there are few places one can't sleep, but none so unlikely and so precarious as the back of a cow. Bob might have said and none so warm and so comfortable.

The technique was like this: Step astride the cow facing the rear, yes the tail end, fold your arms under your chin and firmly wedge your elbows against the pin-bones of the beast *[hip bones]* then cross your ankles over the beast's neck. You are now reclining on a soft animal mattress giving off 300 watts of heat. Nice.

Such familiarity with bovines doesn't always pay dividends, as young Bob always believed it was from the cows he caught 'Ring Worm'.

They had seven or eight cows at Goodshill, one house Cow and the others to provide milk for calf rearing. Ring worm was common in cattle and although this irritation is not an actual worm but a fungal infection it does get under the skin of humans too. With the cattle the treatment was to scrub the area with a wire brush until it bled and then paint it over with iodine. It goes without saying even the cattle found it unpleasant.

Bob's dose of ring worm was on his torso, around his waist, and local folk lore decreed that should the worm completely embrace the body *'you're a dead-un'*. Of course Bob wasn't impressed by old wives tales but they may nevertheless have influenced him to visit the doctor, who politely asked. *'And how do you treat the cows when they get it?'* Bob explained the method but added with a strong note of caution that he hoped the treatment for human's wasn't the same.

Although young Bob could scrub the ring worm off an infected animal knowing the beast was being subjected to discomfort he was doing it for the animals own good and therefore felt no qualms about it. But for all his toughness and his cheeky exterior he was in some ways overly soft and sensitive; indeed an enigma for his chosen occupation. Young Bob could at a pinch, gut a rabbit. He could not draw a fowl neither could he watch the hunt collect a fallen beast; yet he could kill with his hands the countryside's enemy number one, the fox.

In later years when living at Millpond farm, Evelyn tells the story of the Pied Wagtails that started to build their nest on the inside of their old tractor next to the radiator. Bob always made sure he parked in the same place every time he used it right up until the day the hen bird laid its first egg when the pair was left alone to incubate and fledge their young. Being without the tractor was nothing compared to Bob's concern over these little birds. On another occasion Bob shot a Jay he knew was raiding a Chaffinch's nest in their garden hedge, it had a tiny living bald little chick in its beak when he picked it up. He restored the chick to its nest and as far as anyone knows it lived on to be fully fledged. As Evelyn says, 'Bob always looked out for the 'underlings' as he called them, the predators had to watch out for themselves.

Bob would never go ferreting after February because there were so many baby rabbits about and even chastised the dogs for bringing home young rabbits, how they were supposed to know the difference was rather tough on them.

Looking after the stock has to be done at weekends so there's no clocking off at the farm gates and not coming back until Monday. Of course everybody in the country knows that but it may come as a surprise to some that farm work is a sort of none stop shift work for those who want to get away once in a while. Young Bob had an arrangement with his brother Michael that they looked after the stock at Goodshill on alternate weekends. To illustrate the naivety of some towns folk, one weekend when Michael was on duty, for want of a better word, he took with him for company his current mate the Pop Group member Peter Noon of Herman and the Hermits, remember 'There's a kind of hush & We're into something good.?' Michael recalls the incredulous fascination on his mates face as he watched him drawing milk from the cow, squeeze by squeeze, squirt by squirt. Finally he said unbelievably, '*and I thought milk came from a bottle.*'

Another casual farm hand of old Bob's was a man named Jacko Collison. Now Jacko reckoned he was as good with animals as any of the local veterinarians and one of his favourite cure-alls was a cream he called Z.E.B. cream. The origin and ingredients of this potion were a secret known only to Jacko and although he administered it remorselessly throughout the livestock under his care; none ever seemed to be the worse for it. Whether it cured them was of course another matter, but Jacko worked on the principle that if they got better it was due to the cream.

But Jacko's sights were always aimed higher than the lower order animals. If he could persuade a fellow human to try it on a graze, or any aching part of their anatomy for that matter, then he would. Now, old Bob's wife Dodo was a fair to middling tennis player and it came to Jacko's attention that she had hurt her knee playing the game recently, so, armed with his little tub of ZEB cream he set off up to the farm house where earlier he had seen Dodo dozing in the sun.

It must be said that it was never Jacko's intention to risk job, or reputation by assaulting his employer's wife, but his manner of approach left very much to be desired. For Dodo the attentions of the hired help breaking into her slumbers where, who knows, she may have been winning at Wimbledon or running off with Ilya Nastasi in her dreams, to suddenly find Jacko kneeling before her applying his magic potion to her knees was a familiarity too far.

'*Wot you doing you dirty rascal?*' She protested, pulling her dress down to her shins with both hands.

'This ere cream'll cure them knees o'yorn Do, didn't mean nothin else!'

Both Jacko and Dodo survived the experience and as was usual with his famous ZEB cream; her knees got no worse. There were however a few nudges and winks as to whether Jacko really was trying her on a bit.

From time to time amongst herds of cattle there came the infestation that brings with it 'bovine scours' which to the uninitiated is Cows diarrhoea. This rather messy ailment was given its time to run through the herd and clear up as naturally as it arrived. In the summer the excreta used to cake on the thick hide of the legs and tail of the animals, forming hard crusts which cracked and fell off, but not always.

Cow dung has certain qualities recognised by our forefathers but long since lost into the gap which is time itself; sometimes called progress. They used to mix the dung with clay to give it flexibility in the days of daub and wattle walls and if you have ever tried to wash it off your car after splashing though the stuff, then it goes without saying it certainly registers high on the 'strong & clingy' scale.

Jacko's ZEB cream wouldn't cure the scours but he was on the look out for a sore bit to dab it on when one day just to have a closer look he took hold of the tail of one of the beasts, and to his astonishment the tail came off in his hand.

'Oh Bob, Bob!' he shouted, *'the casings come off, the casings come off!'*

In a panic now as he'd intended to pick off the hard set casing which formed on the beast's tail, but in this rare case the circulation had been cut off for so long the tail came off as well.

For all the value of Jacko's administrations there were times when young Bob had to call in the vet. Being a small farmer, small in this case meaning not well off, young Bob couldn't afford anything like those, what he might say, new fangled iron things they calls a 'Crush'. A crush is a cow-sized cage which holds the beast still whilst the vet examines it, so, only if you had a hundred head would you ever be able to justify one of those. In young Bob's case the beast would have to be rounded up before hand and tethered. To say that Bob was dragged around the field 'James Herriot' fashion would be easily understood by followers of that particular TV vet. For the benefit of those who were not, a brief explanation will suffice. Young Bob had suffered something similar to the *'I haven't got all day Mr Luck'* comment already, and although never impressed by impatience was doing his utmost to emulate a cowboy by throwing a loop of rope over the suffering bullock's horns. Determined not to let the beast go he ran behind the bucking animal thinking it would soon tire after which he could then lead it sedately back to the vet. Alas the sick animal found reserves of strength from its panic or its toothache or whatever ailed the wretched thing. Young Bob had mistakenly slipped his arm through a loop in the rope determined not to lose his grip. This was fine until the moment he tripped. Unable to let go, the animal then dragged him at full speed like an out of control toboggan through all the mud and cow dung in its path until it was exhausted, when to Bob's exasperated and breathless disgust it was calmly tended by the Vet.

The French Miners Band - 1956

It was about 1954 when Myxomotosis struck the South East of England, well it didn't so much strike as it was spread with enthusiasm by farmers long troubled by rabbits which they regarded as pests. There were stories in the press about Scottish farmers coming down to England to take home infected corpses, rabbit skins and anything they could they thought would effectively spread the disease on their own farms back home.

Of course as always money was the main driver because the losses to the emerging corporate farms could be counted in hundreds of acres, little did they realise the rabbit would bounce back; they should have of course because nature always does. There were stories, yes once more in the press, of how rabbits were now living above ground, no, not exactly in trees but clears of burrows. The papers carried details of this man made disease and explained how the parasites hosted by the rabbits ensured its rapid spread accounting for millions of deaths. Everywhere the roads were littered with corpses and dying animals.

Real country people, small holders, game keepers, the little people of the countryside weren't too sure about the introduction of the disease; it wasn't natural and therefore could spell disaster.

Young Bob was, like all small farmers, in the middle of all this. It certainly put an end to his ferreting, indeed it was no good keeping ferrets anymore, and as to Evelyn's mother Gladys, probably no one for miles could set a snare like she could; well it put a stop to that too; a not inconsiderable set back considering the amount of rabbits eaten by some country families.

Evelyn, just as her mother had before her, recalls skinning gutting and jointing as many as twelve rabbits at one time, soaking them in brine to bleach the meat. Rabbits were the staple protein of the day in the country.

The so called little country people, small farmers, small holders and their employees ate more rabbit than they did chicken, Now they would need to afford other meat because despite the government's reassurance about there being no danger from the rabbits flesh, no self respecting country man would eat anything he'd shot or wired without seeing it had a clear bright eye, whatever the game. A diseased rabbit was just that and no way would it ever reach the pot as it wasn't worth wasting a cartridge on.

To young Bob this disaster was no big deal; he couldn't influence it anyway. One thing was certain he would ***never ever*** eat rabbit again.

That same year Tenterden received into its bosom the ninety strong 'Miners Band' from Sains-en Gohelle in France, a band of some distinction, calling itself 'Harmonie de la Fosse' *[literally a pit wind band.]* A band born of a mining community just as they are in the north of England; the likes of Brighouse and Rastrick. Tough working men with music flowing through their veins, proud, sometime hard drinking fellows, come to England to give the people a musical treat.

They had come on the invitation of the Tenterden Working men's Club, young Bob's watering hole, to parade the high street and give two concerts. The Kent Messenger reported that they were received with enthusiasm, although one may think also, with just a little curiosity in their style of dress. There was no disguising the origins of the band for as part of their uniform they wore their miner's helmets, somewhat reminiscent of the British Tommies steel helmet and were led at the head of the parade by three miner's wives carrying miner's lamps and willow baskets. At ninety strong this was a powerful band.

Miners as you may be aware are often hard, nay big, drinkers, simply out of the fashion of their work. Hard dusty work under ground makes for a good thirst on the surface. This then was the connecting force between young Bob and the French miners. At some stage after their marching music, after they had entertained the crowded streets of Tenterden, they paused for refreshment as guests of the WMC before dispersing to allotted digs as guests of families around the town. Young Bob was a social being in a big way. He loved people for themselves, their peculiarities, their social-ness and in this case their amitié. As always though he never missed the chance for a bit of fun and taught many of these miners the up to date toast of the region by raising his glass and shouting 'lead in yer pencil!' which the miners mimicked with gusto.

Of course although now a long dead expression 'lead in your pencil' had numerous connotations then, not least of which, alluded to the functions of the male anatomy. This was okay in the working men's club because these French lads didn't know what they were saying and is no different to the coach load of English engineers who on a tour of Sweden taught their driver who had no English what so ever, to say 'shut f****** door' with no guarantee that the next coach load might be from an English convent. Bob had counted on getting away with it like always, but two of these French miners were staying with them at Goodshill, and his mother poured them both a drink with their meal. You've guessed. With timing better than the two Ronnies they raised their glasses and shouted... 'Lead in yer pencil!'

So it was that an unlikely friendship was forged between a Kent farmer and not one but several French miners. Part of this amalgam was no doubt the Cider offered along with the fine fare served up by Dodo. The other common denominator running through the group as a whole was a mutual love of football, not exactly Bob's cup of tea, but the friendship prospered and the result was an invitation back to France a few months later with a football team.

Bob made the journey to Sains-en-Gohelle where he and his mates were given VIP treatment, town mayor, councillors, band the lot. Not finding the French Bistro's quite up to the style of the Black Horse nor the piquancy of their wine as mellow as his own cider never came into the equation, as they were plied with generous amounts of French Champagne from the moment they arrived. For the footballers among them this was not the best precursor for the game.

Bob was paired off with Jimmy French and allocated digs in a farm two miles outside the town. Jimmy relates that they took with them a five piece dance band from Maidstone and although the French too had a band playing music turn a-bout so to speak, the French couples, strangely, seemed only to want to dance when the English band played. The evening spent in the French equivalent of the Village Hall with the miners and their wives was exceedingly convivial and needless to say Bob and Jimmy had rather a lot to drink.

It was a Canadian gentleman from the war graves commission who decided they would need taking to their digs at the farm, leaving them outside the door at the dead of night in total darkness.

They had been told where they could find the door key which they found without trouble but alas the light switch presented some difficulty. They were billeted at the top of a flight of wooden stairs and the two inebriated visitors, unsteadily feeling the walls for the switch, breathing heavily, probably burping and shushing each other in an effort to preserve some sort of English dignity stumbled up the staircase on their hands and knees and into their bedroom.

At this point Bob announced he must have a fag and infuriatingly had to repeat the performance by going down stairs again for a match.

Fifty years ago two grown men sharing a bed held no connotations of any sort whatsoever but nevertheless Jimmy was to have his leg pulled in the ensuing weeks. The men settled down to sleep off their excesses of the day side by side in a French bed in a French farm, one has to guess what was said if anything, sleep being the pressing agent at the time, perhaps they commented on the local lasses or the drink but soon they were both snoring. Half way through the night Jimmy was awakened by the smell of burning and very soon he had shaken Bob awake and the two of them with dawn still not on the horizon were batting the sheets and blankets with their hands to put out a fire. Bob it seems had fallen asleep with his cigarette still alight.

The dawn came too soon for them both. Bob looking bleary eyed out of the window spotted the lady of the house who looking up asking what they wanted for breakfast. Did they want an omelette? with or without herbs? Jimmy shouted over Bob's shoulder yes, or Oui! perhaps. The omelette was duly served up and to Bob's horror it was bright yellow and green. No way could Bob in his delicate state have contemplated that and so he went without, thinking anyway, that he'd make up for it at dinner.

Just before dinner Jimmy and Bob were sat chatting in the kitchen with its warm ambience and cooking smells tantalizing Bob's, by now, growling stomach. Their host, the lady of the house, came in and opened two bottles of red wine, then picking up an oven cloth pulled open the oven doors drew out a large tray containing a number of sizzling rabbits. The heat of the hot appetizing air flooded over them. Bob looked at the rabbits an expression of alarm on his face Madame poured the red wine over the rabbits and pushed the doors closed again. '*Wot's she done that for?*' Bob asked incredulously.

'*Ter kill of all those myxomatosis germs in them rabbits.*' Jimmy replied jokingly.

'*Ughrr! I'm not avin any of that!*' said Bob. And he didn't.

Whenever Bob was presented with short rations he had an expression. '*Enough for two if one goes without.*' No doubt Jimmy would have a good tuck in as Bob wouldn't face the rabbit.

For years after this trip to France Jimmy was to suffer the '*Here's my old sleeping partner.*' comments from young Bob, followed often by, '*We used ter sleep cheek ter cheek both facing the walls he he!.*' Every time he went into the working men's club.

Dogs and Terriers

When young Bob helped Frank Witherden, the same Frank Witherden who suggested he'd make a good jockey, he looked after Frank's Beagle pack. Not so much looked after them, more actually hunted by them. It may seem odd to country readers to find a few couple Beagles in such a heavily wooded part of the county, but there they were and it fell to young Bob to set off in advance dragging a lure of a dead rabbit or aniseed soaked rags for them to hunt. It seems that Frank was intent on Bob being in a chase of some sort, even if it was not to be a Steeple chase.

Bob and Evelyn were keen on terriers and bought their first Jack Russell terrier from Mrs Deeds', wife of the then Sir William 'Bill' Deeds*[now Lord Deeds]* the conservative Member of Parliament and editor with the Times newspaper.

The Jack Russel Pack with friends

This bitch Vicky was to be the foundation of their terrier stock which have hunted and shown with such brilliant success ever since.

A Tale of Three Vicky's

Young Bob's first terrier was a bitch called Vicky, which he later bred from, keeping one of the litter a bitch named Penny. The two dogs made a good team and built a reputation for solving local fox problems which were answered almost on a call out basis for land owners pestered by them.

In the spring of ***1961*** Bob's brother Michael took a call from Benchhill Farm near Appledore , asking, could Bob come out and sort out the foxes on the farm. Bob happened to be away fishing at the time but Michael reassured the caller that he could handle the terriers, so off he went.

When Bob returned it was to hear from his brother that the terriers were lost in the earth and it was now nearly evening. Bob immediately went over to Appledore where he was shocked to discover it wasn't a proper earth. The earth was simply a widened out rabbit burrow which for reasons of cleanliness or danger the vixen had adopted for her cubs, Vixen's having the habit of moving their cubs from the nursery earth at the slightest hint of danger.

Bob called and listened at the earth but there wasn't a sound from his dogs and no clue as to where to dig; it was now dark and nothing could be done except to hope the terriers would come out during the night. The vigil went on all night and friends were called for an early start the next day, deciding to dig a trench around the burrow. It was after midday before Penny was found with two live cubs. The bitch was in a bad way and taken to a nearby house to recover, still they kept on digging and finally some time later Vicky was found dead, along with two dead fox cubs.

Bob was heart broken; he'd had Vicky so long it was like he'd lost part of himself. He insisted she was buried in the fox's earth along with the cubs which is where, he said, she'd want to be. The best way to recover from the loss of a canine friend Evelyn told him was to go out and find a replacement and that's just what they did.

They'd heard that Mike Pelly who was a handler with the Eridge Hunt and lived out near Frant might have a litter, so off they went and met Mike who took them out into a Barn pulled up a few boards and there was a litter of terriers from which they chose Vicky II.

Vicky II turned out to be a first class terrier winning at Romney Marsh Foot Sloggers Club first time out and then the following year winning the championship; at the same time learning her trade with the Foxes

For six years she was to be a good friend, family dog and servant loved by them all especially the two girls Ann and Julie. Once a week Bob used to take the old Austen Gipsy to pick up animal feed and often took the two girls for the ride. On this occasion he had just loaded up when one of the girls said, *'look Dad what we've found.'* Initially he thought it was just white powder down the fronts of their cardigans, to be dusted off, but then to his horror the realization of what it was struck his brain. Strychnine! Old Bob kept the poison in a bottle in the cab of the lorry and, left whilst he loaded up, the girls had been exploring. Panic wasn't one of Bob's failings but there was a need for prompt action which he took, getting them home, as fast as he could to have them changed and made to drink milk to neutralise the poison, the right thing to do in those days. Bob hadn't realized that VickyII had also had a dusting and being a dog had licked it off her coat, sadly passing away soon afterwards.

The next replacement was a terrier named Nippy and pleasant though Nippy was she was also gun-shy and not very much use. She also seemed to have a blind spot for traffic. The first time she was run over by the ring roll and spent twenty four hours in the vets and the last time she was hit on the road at Benenden and to quote Evelyn *'she was no more good after that.'*

Vicky III was bought from the brothers Sid and John Broad at Ticehurst and whilst a fair to middling terrier unhappily developed sugar diabetes and had to be put down at seven years old.

The Collie Cross

Every farm has to have a sheep dog and Evelyn had a Collie Cross which she had had since she left school in 1954 and which, regrettably, she ran over with the farm tractor breaking its leg. Of course there is little more upsetting than running over your own dog and Bob saw to it that it was taken straight to the vet at Cranbrook where they put the leg in plaster. He later observed that the dog seemed not to be healing, favouring the leg which simply hung limply from the shoulder; his concern for the animal forced him to take it back again probably saying that for that money he could have done better himself. This time the vet had to put a metal plate the dog's leg.

On the morning of the day the Collie had to be collected Bob had been digging out some tree roots and a mishap with the spade gave him a real glossy black eye. Evelyn had gone off down to Rolvenden to off-load some sheep when it was time to go, so needing someone to hold the dog he asked Evelyn's sister Joan to go with him. On his way back from Cranbrook to celebrate the return of the Collie gave Bob the excuse, if one was needed, to call at the Cellars Ph.. for a drink. Of course his black eye which had already caused comment at the Vet's and no offer of treatment was the cause of more speculation. *'Come on Bob, how'd ya get the shiner, Too much Cider was it?'* this sort of leg pull was something he'd anticipated. With Evelyn's sister by his side the answer was ready made. *'Aw well yuh see Evelyn caught me out with her sister, thought I was aving a bit of a fling so she poked me in the eye with a short andled brush.'*

As Bob said later, they never believe the truth any way.

Whisky Galore

The replacement for VickyIII was a puppy bought in ***1977*** which the family decided to call Whisky, not, it must be emphasised for any predilection towards the finer spirits in Bob's life. Whisky was so named because she was black and white and thus followed the famous whisky label. Bob's daughter Ann took a dislike to Whisky simply because she, the bitch, had a rough coat, saying she wasn't cuddly like Vicky had been. Vicky had been allowed to sleep on Ann's bed and there had been a strong bond between the dog and the teenager.

This dissatisfaction grew until Bob and Evelyn could stand it no more, after all what was another dog in the house, they had only two and it would be useful to have another terrier with so many foxes about. It seems they were more than willingly pushed into getting another and so when Evelyn's farrier said he knew of a litter over at Faversham they went out and chose a tan and white smooth coated Jack Russell which was to follow the trend by being named Shandy. The colours of Beer and Lemonade if you like.

Fine, so now they were up to strength. Two Jack Russells and the old Collie from Benenden. Alas they had figured without their other daughter Julie. *'I want a puppy. You've got one and Dad's got one and Ann's got one, I want one.'*

Now this was a real problem, not because they couldn't see as parents that it was unfair for her not to have a puppy, but because Bob had said enough was enough in that small house. He'd put his foot down and that was that.

It happened that one of the locals, Bill Waters, who they used to work with for hay and straw from time to time, had a litter born that November. There were two left when Evelyn went to see them and rightly or wrongly she went ahead and chose one. Bob asked her if she'd seen the litter and she said she had adding, bravely, *'you'll be seeing one yourself before long.'* He thought a bit for a while then said *'Well I don't suppose I mind really.'*

It was December before the new puppy came home. Julie had been told she was to get one but assumed it would be in the New Year. It was about late December when Bob met Bill in the Man of Kent pub at High Halden that the deal was sealed over a beer or two and Bob came home with the little puppy in his pocket. When he got home of course, the girls were fast asleep in bed, no drinking man gets home before bed time anyway; but Bob, the man responsible for so many practical jokes, the man who could down a yard of ale in record time, who had won a pewter tankard for eating more pickled eggs than anyone in the county, this tough hard working countryman, crept silently into his daughter's bedroom and gently lay the soft white eight week old bundle of puppy hood against the girl's cheek.

Of course there had to be a name for this new resident and first thoughts were for a drink like her new pals Whisky and Shandy so she very nearly got Jinny, but it was winter and that always prolongs the house training, soon they were dodging little puddles. And also the newcomer was almost pure white save for the tip of one ear, missed, as Evelyn says, by the paint brush of nature. Dodged it like they were dodging the puddles? So, 'Dodger' it was and a right good terrier she was to turn out to be.

You can't be into terriers and not expect to have to dig them out once in a while but Dodger was a real villain in this respect as she would not come out of an earth if she knew Bob or Evelyn were there. She would always finish her business and come out in her own time as if not only the fox was hers but the earth as well. One Sunday morning about eleven -o-clock a fox went to earth with Dodger behind it and by two pm Evelyn had got fed up waiting for her to come out, she had after all to feed the pigs and calves to say nothing of a hundred and one other farm house jobs. She went back later and with some help in the form of George Babbage, Michael Hook and later Peter Johns the Barham's estate game keeper. Between them they dug down to eight feet deep. At times no one could see the top of Evelyn's head as she tunnelled and shouted for the dog. It was eight in the evening when she called for every one to *shush!*, she'd heard something deep in the earth ahead of her. At last out came Dodger after nine hours in a fox's earth.

A similar but much more serious event involving the pack happened in 1985 when Evelyn was Hop Training *[the process of training hop bines up the supporting twine]* for Gerald Orpin. There was nothing to worry about having the pack with her as they amused themselves with a few rabbit burrows nearby as Evelyn worked. The youngest dog Soda, Whisky's daughter, kept coming back to see her and all the time this was happening Evelyn knew things were okay, but she soon realized these visits were more indicative of something else and went to see what the dogs were up to. Following Soda brought her up to what looked like a Badger sett, indeed there was some old turned out bedding but nothing to indicate an active sett. Evelyn called her dogs and almost immediately out came Shandy but no sign of Whisky or Dodger.

Now it is not uncommon for Foxes to adopt old badger workings indeed it has been known for a Fox to share the same earth works. Evelyn assumed this might be the case and that her little pack had gone in after a Fox. She found her self a long stick and poked it down the main sett entrance and was sure she could feel something soft like a dog's body. Calling loudly and generally getting a little angry, it was Whisky who came out first with blood and bite marks on her muzzle. Evelyn's first action when Dodger didn't come out was to take the other dogs home, she didn't want them to go back down the sett and anyway perhaps she'd need a spade. On returning to the sett she didn't have to wait much longer than thirty minutes for Dodger the terrier who wouldn't normally come when she wanted her to, struggled out. Evelyn could see at once that she was badly injured. Her nose was split, parts of her teeth and jaw lost or damaged, her ears in tatters. Evelyn managed to carry the wretched animal 600 yards back to her car and take her off to the vet who without hesitation said she must be put down. No way could Evelyn and Bob, and more to the point Julie, lose their favourite Jack Russell. Leader of the pack, friend, pet.

So the vet sewed her together here and there until she bristled with stitches. Dopey with anaesthetics full of antibiotics and fed soft food for four week Dodger recovered to live on the ripe old age of sixteen years.

Charlie Goodsell's Terrier

A friend of old Bob's by the name of Charlie Goodsell had a little black and white terrier of the Jack Russell ilk that no one can remember the name of. This terrier seemed to take a liking to Goodshill farm and was always hanging around the stock, the Steading, the kitchen, and most of all the two Springer Spaniels belonging to old Bob. The dog didn't seem to have a home to go to, wasn't missed and even though it was Charlie's dog he didn't mind it being away from home either. This was alright most times, but not this summer of 1965 when the builders were busy on the two new cottages at the farm. It was enough to have the builders in without this terrier begging and fussing and generally getting in the way.

The last straw came when old Bob, who wasn't known for his ability for shutting doors, woke up one morning to a great disturbance, not so much noisy but best described as a rude awakening, for one minute he was asleep, and the next, his bed was rocking violently such that half awake he fashioned earthquakes in his mind. Sitting bolt upright, rubbing his eyes in disbelief, there actually on the foot of his bed was one of his Springer's firmly mounted, and in the full throe's of canine copulation by Charlie Goodsell's terrier.

For those not fully acquainted with the dark intricacies of canine intercourse it is the bitch that dictates the scenario, only when she lets go can the dog detach. Whether the fear of old Bob's boot over-rode the ecstasy of the morning is not documented, but some few days later Young Bob took a telephone call from the police station.

'We have a terrier type dog here Mr Luck' the officer said. *'A black and white one, just a bit bigger than a Jack Russell, you lost one have yer?'*

'No mate all our dogs are here. That one sounds like Charlie Goodsell's' Young Bob answered.

'It's got a paint can on its tail.' The Constable continued.

'A paint can?' Bob laughed. *'Really, well we have the builders and painters in here working on the new cottages.'* He replied supportively.

'Mmm, but this can's been tied on.' The officer insisted.

The dog was returned to Charlie Goodsell as large as life and no worse for wear and no one ever owned up to or questioned the paint can incident, or more transparently wondered why the police should think Bob might know the answers.

The Dog Whisky

Whisky was twelve years old when she disappeared one day when young Bob was out shooting in the woods near Millpond farm. He'd taken his gun into the woods and called the dog to go with him. Half way through the morning she ran off after something, Bob assumed a rabbit or a fox and didn't give it a second thought; the dogs were slaves to instinct first and foremost.

When he got back Evelyn asked him where Whisky was and he told her he thought the terrier would be along in a minute. Evelyn's attachment to this terrier over the twelve years they'd had her was stronger than she appreciated. She instinctively wanted to go into the woods and call for her but there was another pressing need, that of Shandy their other terrier who was ailing and needed to be taken to the vet at Tenterden's Highland surgery the then Ogle & Clarke Practice.

To add to her distress, Evelyn's only source of transport was the pony and trap as she had been diagnosed with epilepsy and wasn't allowed to drive a motor car. So it was some few hours later when she returned to be able to go and search the woods for Whisky, alas without success. After a week of using any spare moments to search for her, even to looking in ditches, as Evelyn remembered the discovery of her father's Spaniel being drowned in a ditch years before; the idea of her being lost settled unkindly in her subconscious

Some few weeks following when going about her chores feeding the chicken, with the terriers fussing about her heels as usual, there was Whisky large as life, wet nose, sun shining on the white of her coat.

'There you are Bob, she's back! Those devils up Chennel Park have had her locked up all this time I'll bet.'

Reaching down to fondle Whisky broke the spell, for this

was to be the first of many vivid dreams, dreams which tormented her for two years.

To say that young Bob wasn't sentimental wouldn't be true, he felt the loss too, but his exterior was tougher and he, no doubt, made sympathetic noises until time wore them thin.

The next time Whisky turned up was at the Agricultural show and again later at the Point to Point and down the woods and in the stables. On all these everyday occasions she was real; a real live warm blooded cuddly little terrier living in Evelyn's mind until the cock crowed on the dawn of another day.

The most enduring dream, so real, so life like, where she berates the children for leaving open the kitchen door lest Whisky ran out side. It was a strange kitchen, one she couldn't place, with green doors and unfamiliar things about it. The children did leave the door open, always, time and time again. Each time she ran out to seek her beloved Whisky only to find herself not outside Millpond farm with its fine high views of the woods and across to Goodshill with its happy memories; but out in an unfamiliar street. A street to be searched without success until that spell of sleep was broken.

It was May in 1991 that Evelyn had an hysterectomy and during her convalescence was helped by a very caring Physiotherapist Jo Christian who lived in Hastings. The relevance of this became apparent one morning in that near to wakefulness, that is neither sleep nor consciousness, when even with a little encouragement a nice dream cannot be prolonged, yet a bad dream never seems to want to become detached. There she was in that kitchen with its green doors when in trots Whisky large as life as usual, except this time she rolled over to expose a huge scar on her belly. The shock broke the spell and Evelyn awoke.

This was a black day. Shandy who was fourteen and half years old and who's health had been failing for sometime was to be put down. The old girl wasn't enjoying life and the release was a merciful thing. The date was imprinted on Evelyn's mind ***'The 15th January 1992'*** Wasn't it enough to be joined nightly by dreams of Whisky? Now here was the loss of her playmate two years later on. It was a crucial moment for Evelyn, a revelation indeed in the form of a post card in that very next morning's post.

The cover picture was simple enough. A rose.'Historic Rosa Gallica' a picture to lighten the heart of any gardener. The message too was heartening, from Jo Christian hoping your recovery continues etc..... and the date ***Jan 15th 1992***

Realisation wasn't instant but gradual; The street outside the kitchen with the green doors was at Hastings, the street she'd searched in her dreams so often was actually outside Jo's house. The scar on Whisky's belly was her hysterectomy, and the kitchen, after all those years revealed itself as that of another friend and confidant Veronica Wilson at Woodchurch. Jo Christian couldn't have known about Evelyn's dreams nor of the timing of the vet's visit to Shandy but the action unwrapped the torment of the years since November 1989 when she had searched for footprints around the steamy castles the Badgers dug on that frosty week in the woods where Whisky disappeared.

Young Bob was cut up about Shandy's passing and probably found it hard to reconcile with the new found spirit in Evelyn; but then two years is a long time.

Sea Fishing

When young Bob worked for his Uncle Sid at Smarden 1944 he learned to catch eels with 'lay lines' in the rivers Beult and Sherway which ran through his Uncle's land. This may have inspired Bob's love of fishing.

There was a story going the rounds attributed to Bob's sense of fun which I suppose confirms the sort of humour he had, but also demonstrates how when an individual has this sort of reputation that individual becomes a repository for incidents that really don't belong.

A regular escape from the hard graft of farm work was Bob's liking for deep sea fishing and often he and some of his mates would charter a boat from Dungeness point. The boat would go out into the channel and anchor over one of the wrecks, where they, on a good day would pull in a Conger Eel or two, maybe a Cod and in the summer months hit one of the massive shoals of mackerel.

But this day Bob was said to be out of sorts as he had mislaid his top set of teeth. As a jape one of his mates pulled in on his hook a set of teeth found somewhere on the boat or in his kit. *'Look Bob we've caught your teeth!'* was the exclamation. Bob took the teeth without a smile, popped them in his mouth clenched them firmly together then spat them out, back into the sea where they quickly disappeared. '*Not mine.*' He grunted, to the astonishment of his mates who really thought they were.

Of course like many stories the subject of the story can be turned around to be the object of it and this is the case here for Evelyn affirms quite positively that Bob had his own teeth all his life. It is highly probable that someone else, not Bob lost their teeth, and extremely likely that Bob was the perpetrator of the jape.

On one occasion Bob went off on his deep sea fishing trip with his pals wearing a duffle smock he'd been given. A duffle smock being made like a duffle coat, same stuff, and the same design but with no opening down the front, indeed made like a smock; you might say the forerunner of the anorak. The sea was quite choppy, the deck wet and slippery; predictably, Bob lost his footing, except this time he hit the gunwale and went overboard. Now it was the quick thinking of his mate, local electrician Alan King who was a dab hand at gaffing a conger when the occasion demanded it, plus Bob's new garment which contained the air in such a manner as to keep him afloat that saved the day. But for the smock he may not have stayed afloat long enough to be hooked by the hood of his new garment.

The local Press heard about the incident and wanted to print the story with headlines like. 'Bright spark saves farmer.' But it never hit the streets. Alan did say to Evelyn however, that saving young Bob must be worth a couple of those mallards you have on that pond of yours, to which Evelyn replied. *'If you'd held him under instead of bringing him back home you could've had the lot!'*

Sometimes they sailed out of Rye harbour in a boat owned by Mick Haynes. They started the day, at least four of them, Jim Thompson, Geoff Pay, Jim Jennings and Bob by

Left: Alan King, the man who saved Bob's life.
Right, Young Bob with a Blue Shark weighing 98lb.

meeting at the Vine Inn in Tenterden about six thirty in the morning. The landlord Eddie Hobbs would leave Bob a crate of beer outside the back door to take on their trip and there's no doubt they'd have a few bread rolls to see them through their days fishing. On one of these days Bob wasn't all that fresh, having had a skin full the night before and when Mick dropped anchor about three miles out it was all he could do to keep his eyes open. Not being able to resist the desire to sleep Bob fixed the handle of his rod to the crate of beer, baited his hooks and threw the weights over the side for the tide to take away until the line was stretched out nearly horizontal. Comfortable that all was safe he settled down in the bottom the boat to sleep. Jim Thompson who was often the butt of Bob's jokes suggested they pull in Bob's line and tie on one of his bottles of beer. The others agreed and when the line was taut again they shouted to Bob, '*waken up Bob you've got a bite!*

Bob shook at the calls for him to tend his line. He had been in a nice sleep, a recuperative sleep, the sort of sleep not to be interfered with. He looked at the blue sky and scudding clouds and put his hand on the gunwale to steady him self. '*Wha..what?*' he asked.

'*You've got a bite! His mates chorused.*'

Bob started to reel in the heavy weights against the run of the tide encouraged by his friends. At last up popped the weights followed by the bottle of precious brown ale to great guffaws from his pals. Then just as Bob reached out for the beer bottle it fell off and disappeared in an instant. Funny or not funny it is always safe for a group to laugh at the downfall of a single individual, never the reverse. '*What silly bugger wasted one of my bottles of beer?*' he shouted at them all, his eyes still flinching at the daylight. By then everyone was intent on watching their rod.

There was another occasion when they left Dungeness to go fishing only to find they had forgotten their bait. The boat was rented to some chaps from London and Bob had difficulty cadging bait from them, okay so once you've got a bite you can cut it up for bait but it's never the same as lug worm and these strangers had tons of it. No matter how Bob approached the issue they sort of handed over one at a time, and this niggardly attitude was beginning to get up Bob's nose.

It was to Bob's advantage that the sea cut up a bit after they had been out about an hour and the two strangers were soon looking just a little queasy. The boat was bow into tide the anchor rope out taught and the men's lines almost horizontal. In this situation the bow was lifting and falling with the sea, one minute those at the stern were higher than those in the bow the next they were lower. Earlier someone had pulled up a squid, not a big one but big enough for Bob to pick up from the bottom of the boat saying, *'time for lunch isn't it? Ave you lads tried squid with yer sandwiches?'* Bob took out his knife and sliced off one of the squid's tentacles, then made sure everyone was watching before dropping it down his throat. Bob had only to watch their eye's, he made a point of letting the tentacle dangle from his lips before chewing it with gusto and finally swallowing it. That was all it took. Grabbing the gunwale of the lurching boat the first stranger threw up over the side into the white horses running past. *'you won't be needing your bait then mate'* Bob remarked and the problem was solved.

Rye Harbour

All the Luck family used to go down to Rye harbour in the summer to go fishing on the shore, picnic, drink a few bottles of cider and get a bit of fresh air. On one occasion when they were all expected and yet arrived without young Bob, old Bob told his mate Graham Saunders, the lad, young Bob would be along later as he had some things to do.

Nothing more was thought of this and they duly arrived and all had a good time and went home again; that is except for Mrs Ledger wife of the Smarden butcher who couldn't get her car to move, the engine would go but the car wouldn't budge. She called her husband who had the same trouble. It was a large car, a very prestigious Humber Super Snipe, indicative of his success as a family butcher. Of course the Lucks had gone but Ledger recruited Graham's help and discovered that 'someone' had jacked up the car and stood it on apple logs so that the rear wheel just cleared the ground. Between them and with great difficulty they managed to get the car off the logs and go home.

Nothing was said of the incident, which is always an anti climax for the perpetrators, however one day Mr Ledger asked old Bob if he had any old barrels as he wanted them to make flower-tubs for outside his shop. [Evelyn's version described this request as the barrels were needed for scalding the pig's hides]. But no matter, the barrels were duly supplied... 'complete with a dead fox inside each one'. It wasn't as if you could look inside the barrel and see the fox, that would have been too straight forward, these were complete barrels, old Bob had gone to the trouble of removing the head from the barrel, slackening the bands and staves then refitting the head.

So here we have a case of practical jokers, going to such extremes of effort to affect a joke, like father like son. Young Bob jacks the car up, old Bob puts the dead foxes in the barrels, and they do this to friends, not even rivals in business. The psychology is difficult, but everyone took it as read, this is how it was, hard workers, hard players; and they took retaliation with the same understanding.

Mr Ledger was not very well suited with the dead foxes in the gifted barrels, and yet again he let things ride for a while until some weeks later, old Bob ordered several pounds of sausages.

When they sat down to eat them they were unable to cut them in half for each one had in it inserted length-wise a thick hard wooden butcher' skewer.

The family said afterwards Ledgers sausages were the only sausages they'd known with a back bone, but were still easier to fillet than Bignell's kippers.[Evelyn's family you will recall had a fish shop in the high street.]

In Tenterden Bob and Ray Millen often stopped to buy fish and chips from the van owned by Horace Moore, this probably after a few pints in the Vine across the road from where Horace used to park his van, where the old Midland Bank, now the HSBC is. Of course it wasn't illegal then and quite a few people would gather to buy and eat their chips al fresco. Horace aided by his nephew Dave Moore would be quite busy at closing time, so busy indeed, that they didn't notice young Bob lying under their van stuffing every discarded old chip paper up the exhaust pipe.

Horace was very proud of his chip van, he kept it clean and nice, but he was obsessive and it must have been this, *'don't rock the van, keep yer hands off'*. attitude that provoked young Bob that evening. The upshot was that when Horace and Dave drove away at the end of their night's work it was to the loud bang from their exhaust system which reportedly fell in the road behind them.

Accident Prone

Not only was Bob accident prone, but liquid was often involved, whether outside his body or inside, often both. Unlike the great cartoonist Batemen who once decreed that whilst it was always safe for a crowd to laugh at the misfortunes of one person, it was never safe for one person to laugh at the misfortunes of a crowd. Young Bob like his father had the sense of humour and spirit to smile at his own misfortune and not only that, had the added turn of phrase for such occasions.

The later story of the Crit Hall fire engine attributed to old Bob is a case in point, but there are others, like the evening young Bob went out dressed in one of the few suits he treasured, had a few drinks and coming home to Millpond farm in the dark missed his way and ended up immersed in the Pig swill. Of course there were no witnesses to the ducking, no one there to laugh or commiserate '*a propos*' Batemen; But in he walks looking and smelling like a drowned rat saying to Evelyn that he'd fallen, '*In Frittenden Harbour!*' .*[Frittenden being ten miles inland from Benenden and nowhere near the sea.]*

Those unfamiliar with the farm work of the day, especially dairy cows may not appreciate the affinity the cow-man has with his bovine charges. At the risk of seeming indelicate, Cows defecate from the height of about four feet and their faeces are never ever solid. It's a bit like the old joke of '*can you make a noise like a cow with a pack of cards?*' well, no one can see how one can make a 'Moo' sound can they? But if you drop the cards flat in sequence on a flat surface then the noise is like a cow, defecating.' Got it?

To get back to the point, Bob never wore good clothes about the cow-shed for he was bound to end up covered in cow muck. This meant he was always the ready recipient of 'hand me down' clothes. Being of small stature most clothes would fit, albeit badly, but that didn't matter. He was on one occasion given some rather nice shirts which as usual were too long, indeed the tails came down to his knees, but so what, tucked in they were warm and no bother, until one morning he was taken short and had to bolt quickly for the hedgerow. The unfortunate if indelicate details at this juncture need not be related but suffice to say the tails were forgotten when they should have been remembered and it was a very sorry Bob who insisted that certain tailoring would be appropriate before he would wear those *'Bloody Dung hammocks'* again.

Often, rotten trees, nuisance trees, stumps and the like were taken down and chopped up for firewood. Never a shortage, indeed an ongoing thing on most farms in the region. One large tree overhanging the pond at Crit Hall was scheduled to be taken down and Bob had decided that the best way was to fell it into the pond and pull it out with the tractor. He decided much against Evelyn's better judgement to pull the head of the tree out hoping it would swing round, and proceeded to walk up the trunk to tie on the rope despite his wife's remonstrations that pulling it out by the butt was the best way. But what did she know? Three quarters along the trunk the tree rolled, influenced obviously by Bob's weight. There was a moment of equilibrium sustained by Bob's flaying arms accompanied perhaps by '*Whoa whu ahrr!*' until it was lost and he plunged headlong into the water. The woolly hat he used always to wear floated one direction and a weed covered Bob struggled out the other, stinking with black mud and declaring he'd had enough for the day. The tree was later pulled from the pond by the butt.

They say you can tell a good saw miller by a missing finger or thumb. Perhaps then a good tree feller can be told by his narrow escapes. Bob was cutting a heavy hornbeam one day when he misjudged the amount of weight resting on the limb he was removing. It was an awkward cut as the tree laid across the hedge which grew atop a bank with a ditch between. As the bough gave way it rolled into the ditch, knocking Bob over and trapping him underneath, only the concave shape of the ditch saving him from being crushed, but that was not all, for he'd lost hold of the saw which seemed to have a mind of its own revving and smoking just a whisker from his nose.

Dave Turner who had the treasured experience of teaching Bob to drive said Bob ran out of road more often than not and his progress was best recorded in telegraph poles; 'three broke, four bruised.' Indeed one of Bob's earliest encounters with the law was for erratically driving the old Standard van they had at that time. He was stopped near the Man of Kent Ph. But managed to talk himself out of it, telling the officer the steering was wonky.

Most of Bob's accidents were remarkably sustainable, not serious, more messy than anything. However whilst out with the shoot one year about 1950 he vaulted a gate and landed on dry rutted ground and hurt his ankle. He had to be carried home and then taken to the Doctors at Ivy Court. It was then Dr T who examined him and declared the ankle badly sprained and sent him home well strapped up. Unfortunately the ankle was later to give him a great deal of trouble for in 1982 after years of putting up with pain and a permanent swollen ankle he was forced to return to the doctor who referred him to the hospital for X-ray. He was later recalled to the surgery to hear the result which was that his ankle was broken in three places followed by the question and *'who was the doctor?'*

'You were!' replied Bob, with a certain satisfaction. The operation which followed was a triple arthrodesis. This operation involved cutting away the diseased cartilage and fusing the bones together with a resultant loss in mobility in as much as the ankle would go up and down but without lateral movement of any kind. The convalescence was long and painful and Evelyn had to dress a particularly livid wound daily through a little aperture or window as she puts it, left in the plaster cast. His mate Butch Goodsell said his ankle looked as though it had been attacked by a corned beef tin.

It wasn't long before Bob was back to riding his bike again having been banned from driving since 1980 and it was whilst riding into Tenterden one day that he was hit by a van on the main road opposite Turner's Avenue. The van driver had tried to squeeze through between two other vehicles and somehow hooked onto Bob's handlebars throwing him off his bike and into the path of another vehicle. The van driver did not stop but fortunately there were witnesses to the accident. Evelyn received a message to say he had been taken to the Tenterden Club and would she pick him up from there. When she arrived she found him in a dreadful state and with the help of a friend insisted he go to the doctors. Young Bob's reluctance to go speeding off to the Doctors at every sign of hurt or illness was common to his generation but may have been influenced by his recent experience with his ankle. Suffice to say Bob had a broken collar bone two broken ribs a badly jarred hip and bruising stretching from his ear to his foot. Evelyn says she has never seen such bruising.

The woman driver of the van was traced to Rainham. She insisted she wasn't even in Tenterden on that day and it wasn't until the eleventh hour that she changed her plea to guilty to driving without due care and attention. Bob was later awarded £10,000 compensation. In 1986 he had to have his hip replaced, certainly exacerbated by the damage sustained in the accident. This was carried out by the same surgeon who had done his ankle some years before and cost him nearly £4.000 privately at St Saviours Hospital Hythe.

It was very soon after his operation when he had a visit from one of his mates Andy Grant from Headcorn who being a good friend and responsible hospital visitor brought along a little refreshment in the form of a gallon of his home made cider suitably disguised in a Sarson's vinegar bottle. Of course young Bob couldn't have wished for a more appropriate gift but was naturally worried about the gallon bottle complete with Sarsons label sitting on top of his bedside locker. He telephoned Evelyn immediately fearing the nurses might confiscate the stuff if they knew what it was. He happened to have some Lucozade bottles which he duly topped up with the cider and told Evelyn on the phone to bring a means of further disguising the rest. Now Bob was under strict orders to drink plenty of fluid, they never tell you why, just that you must, but happily this was no hardship for young Bob for every time the nurse asked him if he wanted a cup of tea he replied. '*Er no thanks nurse I'll just have a little of my Lucozade.*'

The operation left him with the need to walk with a stick; crutches for the first few weeks. If there was a plus side to this painful operation it was that it lengthened his previously short leg to something like the length it should be, as one leg had been one and a half inches shorter than the other. None of this stopped Bob participating in his country pursuits especially shooting, however it did affect his balance considerably because on more than one occasion the recoil of the shotgun knocked him flat on his back, no doubt making any other guns in the line distinctly nervous.

One evening whilst living at Millpond farm Bob announced he was having chest pains, insisting to Evelyn that it was probably a heart attack. It wasn't until the doctor examined him and diagnosed a cracked rib that he remembered exactly what he had done. Most farms habitually pile up the dung from the stock and chickens in a mound, a midden traditionally; this concentrates the matter and encourages heat and decomposition. As the pile grows so a plank is provided to run the wheel barrow up and thus each new load can be delivered neatly to the top, simple. Bob was, earlier that day pushing a loaded wheel barrow, the plank was wet and slippery and a little momentum was required to reach the top, so he took a run at it. He should have remembered Benenden school and his science lessons and that however much momentum you have, just a little friction on the prime mover will be required as the momentum dies. Alas farmers don't worry about such complications. Bob had taken a run at the plank pushing the barrow, got half way up when his feet slipped first one foot after the other, until in his own words he was doing an '*Andy Cap!*' with his legs a blur and the barrow stationary. Exhausted he'd collapsed on the barrow smashing a rib in the process. Evelyn relates that it wasn't to be the last time he'd crack a rib as he slipped in the bathtub some months later doing the same thing on the taps.

It would be about the year 1981 at Millpond Farm with friends, a guy called Bullit and two others, Les and Brian from Rochester way, casual chaps they met over at the Morris's place, Haylands farm when they were over there picking geese one time. They joined up for some ferreting in woods nearby. Bob was setting up the nets prior to slipping the ferret. The bury [burrow] he was working at was covered with stout brambles, so there he was kneeling down slashing at the brambles around the bolt hole one at a time with his knife when the knife slipped and stuck in his thigh. '*Ouch! Bugger.*' Was probably all he said, giving his leg a rub he continued with the nets.

Very soon everyone became aware of the dark red saturation down his leg and even the bloody footprint he was leaving as he moved about the warren. '*You ought to do something about that, give it a clean up, and put something on it hey.*' Said Evelyn, who'd seen him do it.

'*Nah it'll be alright till we finish ere.*' Bob replied, and slipped the ferret, sitting down to wait. At this point someone produced a piece of kitchen tissue which bob pushed through the hole in his trousers more an act of appeasement than anything else.

At last the burrow was cleared and they all trouped off back to Evelyn's kitchen where she sat Bob down and helped him ease off his Wellington boots, first the dry one then the other. To her amazement it was full of blood. Then Bob dropped his slacks to reveal his bloody leg where blood oozed from the small wound in his thigh. When Evelyn gingerly tugged the tissue away a fine jet of crimson blood shot upwards almost reaching the ceiling. Bob had nicked his femoral artery and had been working on as though it had been a mere scratch.

The thought of treatment on such things horrified him, not out of fear, he wasn't afraid of anything, more a squeamishness. They had to take him to the William Harvey Hospital on this occasion for the wound to be treated; hydrogen peroxide in those days, before it was stitched up.

Strangely this treatment led into the subject of drink as sure enough Bob had with him one of his so called 'hand grenades'. These were the cans of Barley Wine he had taken to drinking since the cider was no longer available. The male nurse who had attended to Bob noticed the can. *'Oh you like a drink now and then do you mister Luck?'* He asked.

'Oh yes I have to ave one of these now and then.' He replied. No more was thought of the incident until some time later when Bob was in for attention to his ankle and the same nurse recognised him. 'Oh I remember you. You're the man who likes Barley wine aren't you?' before Bob could reply the nurse continued. *'We'll see what we can do about that then Mr Luck.'* And he picked up the clip board from the foot of the bed and wrote down barley wine, three pints per day for Mr Luck.

Bob couldn't believe it, mentally rubbing his hands together and feeling real sorrow for those patients he'd seen with notes 'nil by mouth.' thank God it wasn't him.

Next morning it was a fresh faced young female nurse on the ward. She looked at Bob's clip board and smiled at him, saying. *'Don't forget Mr Luck it is most important to drink plenty after an operation. I see you are to have three pints a day..'* Bobs eyes lit up. *'Lemon barley water, see you finish it.'*

Bob had pet dislikes and once threatened to shoot one of his pals if he didn't let go a grass snake he said he had hidden in his shirt. You see, he didn't like snakes but he didn't like to see the creature imprisoned either. He disliked doctors, hospitals, men with pony tails and politicians; of the latter he said they were like a hand of bananas. *'They arrive green turn yellow and not a straight one amongst them'.*

His ankle disability had left Bob more than a little unsteady on his feet and one day after falling over the cat he recounted to Evelyn the story of the teacher at Benenden who asked them all if they had pets and what their names were. One little boy had a rabbit called Tom another a budgie called Billy, a series of dogs names followed until finally there was the little girl who told teacher her daddy always called their pet cat 'cooking fat!'.

Hastings - 1961

A common so called hunting ground for young people in the 1960's was Hastings, the '*in place*' for good food and a bit of fun. One popular place for entertainment was the Carlisle; a licensed premises half way along the promenade existing to this day. In those days they served beer had a dance band and often a floor show, so it attracted good crowds especially in the summer season.

Bob and Evelyn were Saturday night regulars for a while and may even have been tempted to pop in on Wednesdays after their Cider deliveries. Like most young people in the sixties they were caught up in the mania for rock music such as Elvis Presley and the wild groups which made that decade so exciting. Dress for most would have been the tight trousers and crepe soles, perhaps even a velvet collar and longer jacket even winkle pickers, whilst the girls sported the flared skirts and stiletto heels; maybe even a bouffant hair do.

But not so for Bob and Evelyn. They were country people and there isn't a stock man, dairy man or plough man, who would have felt at home in such apparel. Of course they pandered to the needs of fashion in small ways, perhaps Bob would have grown his side burns and even dared a kipper tie but that would be it. Country folk aren't that daft.

One Saturday, Bob, Evelyn, her sister Joan, John Sims known as Simbo and another friend Pete Miller all went off to Hastings for an evenings dancing and a few pints at the Carlisle

Bob had a mate called Stan who for some unexplained reason was always called Butch. Butch had been seeing a young nurse from Benenden Chest hospital and the news leaked out that he'd got her in the family way. Now it so happened one of the props used by the band at the Carlisle was a very large and rather dated pram. The pram was painted according to the taste of the band in bright colours with a number of slogans such as; *'Dig this!' 'Don't you rock me daddy'O!' 'I love Elvis'* and the like.

It hadn't escaped Bob's notice that such a pram might be useful to his mate, after all Butch was going to be a daddy'O himself. Bob knew the band well, indeed he was on first name terms and so seizing the opportunity when there was a lull in the evening he offered to buy the pram. The band leader asked why they would want to buy it; after all, it was no longer really an acceptable item in terms of infant transportation due to its garish decorations. Guessing there was a hidden purpose behind the need they insisted to be let-in on the ruse in Bob's mind and he was forced to explain. .To Bob's surprise the band gave him the pram, enjoying his idea for a prank as much as he did.

For those who don't carry a street map of Hastings the Carlisle is about a mile from the old black fisherman's huts which is where they had left their transport that evening. Transport being the operative word as 'old Ford 5cwt.van' would be a better description. Someone had to push this rather bright, nay very loud, pram through the streets of Hastings and as if wanting to attract attention Bob got inside it letting his legs dangle over the sides while the rest took it in turns to push.

The dimensions of the old 5cwt. Vans were pretty tight, some will remember them being used by the Royal Mail as was, small and practical. The five revellers looked at the vehicle that had brought them here to Hastings in the early evening and wondered in their bemused state how they and this large pram were ever going to get home.

It was elected that Simbo, the most inebriated of the five, would play the part of the baby and thus he was unceremoniously plonked into the pram and the pram squeezed into the back of the van. Bob was unworried, as the driver he was sure of a seat. Pete, gallant as ever grabbed the passenger seat leaving the choice between the area between the two seats or Pete's lap which was immediately chosen by Evelyn's sister Joan. So there was no choice for Evelyn other than to spend the journey astride the gear lever.

The journey was alive with laughter tinged with serious concern going up the steep London road as they might lose baby Simbo down the hill and into the sea; for every time they braked the pram surged forward and every time they accelerated the pram hit the back doors loudly.

Apart from that the journey was uneventful save for a comfort stop at the Hexden Levels for the men to have a scatter or as Bob called it *'for baby Simbo to have his nappy changed'* It was about mid night before they arrived at Swain Road St Micheals where they delivered the wonderfully colourful pram to the lawn right outside the window of Butch's home.

Of course they all wished they could have been there to see the effect of their jape, after all they went to enormous trouble to obtain the pram and could only imagine what would happen when Butch looked out of the window the following morning and what his parents might say. It was Pete Miller who took a stroll that way the following day to find some young lads using the pram on the hilly section of Swain Road as a bogey cart, which was somewhat of an anti climax.

Butch himself let out the real truth by declaring he'd whip the hide of the guys who did it, and he'd a pretty good idea who, but they were empty words, exposing his embarrassment.

Bob and Evelyn had heard that Butch's parents didn't get on very well at all and rumour had it that when they weren't talking to one another they tied a note to the collar of their Jack Russell for the other to find, that being their only communication. And so as the pram joke grew old and word spread about, like most stories it was exaggerated. Easy to imagine the note reading on the discovery of the pram on the lawn, '*huh like father like son!*' or '*was there something I should know dear?*'

Butch never married his nurse from Beneden Chest Hospital and the pram ended up as a toy for the local kids, but there was an irony young Bob and Evelyn couldn't be aware of. If Butch had only known he'd have kept the pram for them.

Hastings keeps cropping up as a key location in young Bob's life Wednesday's particularly as that was the day he did the Cider run to the customers there. He also spent time at the fish market and would buy boxes of fish to sell door to door when he got back to Tenterden. He was cheeky enough to offer those he couldn't sell to the local fish mongers who no doubt wondered why they could never sell any them themselves.

On one occasion he was so hot after having had a few drinks in the town with his mates that he went down to the sea front threw off his clothes and plunged into the sea completely naked. That was fine and refreshing except that his mates often the butt of young Bob's jokes took their opportunity to get their own back. Not only did they steal his clothes but threw stones at him if he tried to come out of the water. It wasn't until a crowd had gathered, happily leaning on the railings, that he was allowed to pull his trousers over his wet buttocks to the jeers and applause of the onlookers.

Michaels Wedding - 1961

Young Bob's brother Michael got married in 1961. At that time he drove an Austin A60 pick-up which he had valetted and polished avidly for the occasion.There was no way his vehicle, used daily on farm business, was going to look as though that's what it did.

Bob had quietly noticed the work his brother was putting into it and made plans to doctor it up a bit himself for when the couple came out of the reception ready in their best going away outfits, off on their honeymoon.

Of course it wasn't unusual for this to happen and the tin cans tied to the chassis and the toilet rolls glued to the coach work were after all one of the last shots in the mating game. The aim was to let everyone from here to wherever their destination was that here were a newly married couple. Confetti down the back of the grooms shirt and in the suit cases and wallets and handbags, this was the norm. Maximum exposure, maximum embarrassment, that was the aim.

Of course who in the whole world would you expect to know Bob Luck best, if not his brother Michael.

Bob had gone further than most would on such an occasion, for he had also bought a couple of tins of Kitty-Kat, opened up the bonnet and spread the delicious meaty substance over the manifold of the engine.

At last the happy couple were released from their reception to the cheers of family and well wishers, they walked, to Bob's astonishment, straight past Michael's beloved pick-up and into old Bob's Austin Westminster to drive off to their secret destination. It is not recorded but there is not the slightest doubt that Michael would give his big brother, young Bob, a sly grin as he slipped the big car through the gears.

For once Bob had been predictable. His brother knew him better than he would have guessed and the joke was on him. But it hadn't ended there as the pick-up had to be driven to Goodshill farm and first of all Evelyn had to be dropped off at her home. The vehicle he had so diligently decorated had to be just as diligently divested of the toilet rolls and tin cans. But what of the Kitty-Kat?

With a cavalier *'oh that'll burn off before we get home.'* Remark, Bob set off with Evelyn sat beside him in her best wedding reception clothes.

Although Bob worked around animals and was all too familiar with the gory, one might say shitty environment, he had no stomach for the obnoxious putrefaction that was being wafted through from the engine and very quickly threw up over the dash board. By this time his brother and his new bride would be miles away in their father's car but, like the Kitty-Kat on the manifold their ears too would be burning.

It was about 1961 when young Bob and his drinking partners were doing what all young men did about that time, going to the dancing, generally socializing; going out for a drink or a meal as Friday night in Tenterden probably was much the same as anywhere else in the country. This particular Friday night was invaded by incomers from Ashford hell bent on making trouble. Quite a mêlée was going on outside the Town Hall late in the evening and the local bobby PC Ron Jackson was under siege. Anyone who thinks two thousand and three is bad it's not the year but the martial mentality of certain young men that makes each decade the same in terms of drunken disorder. These guys, louts, hooligans, call them what you like were armed to the teeth. They had bike chains, lead piping, hammers and jemmies not to mention the fencing spile they were attacking PC Jackson with. Young Bob his friends Neil Warwick and David Turner had come on the scene in their good clothes, in good spirits too, when there, happening on the pavement was this rather evil confrontation.

That was their local bobby having a bashing, not just any bobby. So in the three of them waded pouncing on the guy with the fencing stake. It was young Bob who grabbed him first and got him neatly in a head lock, but facing backwards. Of course a headlock still leaves the arms and legs free, it's just the head and neck you're squeezing, not the most restrictive of wresting grips and so his victim's arms were thrashing about. Neil Warwick determined to help Bob stepped forward and took a swing at the captive head. It was a first class delivery, Rocky Marciano couldn't have done better, but alas the man moved with a split second to spare and Neil's fist buried itself into Bob's ribs.

'Ouch! You silly bugger Warwick, I'm on your side!' Shouted Bob and his man squirmed free.

The fight was neither won nor lost moving along the pavement scuffle after scuffle. The gang took flight, dashing for their vehicle. A local trader Dave Stanger, whose father and grandfather ran a Grocer's shop where Webb's Cook Shop now is, threw his trade bike in front of the getaway vehicle to see it wrecked before his eyes. In true keystone cops style young Bob and his cohorts had swelled to posse proportions by now with the addition of Pete Miller and Geof Pay. They gave chase in Bob's van but were stopped by the police at Woodchurch. The police politely appealed to them that perhaps they should take over now.

The case came to Court at Tenteden when the magistrate after sentencing those of the hooligan's before him praised the heroic efforts of those local young men from Tenterden who had gallantly gone to the aid of the Police that night. To avoid retaliation none of our hero's was mentioned by name but this didn't stop them coming back and smashing Neil Warwick's shop window some nights later.

The Burgeoning Romance 1959

Evelyn had known Bob since she was a young girl of about twelve years old and remembers the incident where he swam out to rescue the Spaniel trapped in the lake. She may have been subconsciously impressed by this brave act. She may have feared for him and the dog. It is doubtful at that age if she had thought it foolhardy or romantic even and certainly would not have been attracted by his almost naked body as he was rubbed down with Jack Russell's old great coat.

At some stage the seed of romance was sewn, but like many seeds theirs was a slowly evolving variety, after all there was an eight and a half year difference in their ages and they knew each other mostly through the familiarity of their families.

Evelyn used to do the lookering for her father at Heronden. *[Lookering is a Kentish colloquial term for examining the flock, looking out for foot-rot, maggots, blow fly, lameness and the like.]* This she did on horseback across the levels south of the Newmill channel, dry only in summer and suitable only for marsh sheep in those days. It was the early sixties before the current flood control came into being with the more recent satellite controlled pumps and Archimedes screws.

Then, the marsh was a series of water meadows and dykes which could be relied upon to flood, flood plain fashion, bringing in with it great flights of Mallard to feed in the slops, as the shallow marsh waters were called. It was young Bob's love of duck shooting brought them closer together at this time. Evelyn had a constant eye on the marsh and knew where the fowl were best found. Indeed she and Bob enjoyed their shoots so much she took to putting out barley and other feed to bring the birds in. When the waters started to recede she resorted to, on one occasion, blocking one of the drains to keep the slops up and the duck interested. She recalls also how on the colder days the marsh fog hung heavily over the slops, thick and unmoving; and they with just their heads sticking up above it waiting eerily for the flights.

We are bound to ask at this stage if Evelyn was coveting the duck shooting or trying to keep Bob in tow, but duck shooting doesn't last forever; and it is true to say that about this time they drifted away from each other for a spell of doing their own thing, just seeing each other from time to time.

It was in the fifties that Bob took to going to France on a sort of, if not freebie travel, then certainly cheap travel arrangements through a friend of his Ray Millen and Ray's brother in law Bert Kingsnorth who worked for Silver City Airways at Lydd. The Airways operated out of Lydd air port then called Ferry Field. Their trips were to where ever the cheap seats took them, often Amsterdam, sometimes Paris, Le Touquet and the like. The code words for these sojourns, coined by the wives were 'The boy scouts outing' or 'The choir boys outing.' This implying innocence to a trip that was nothing more than an excuse for a couple of days on the town and a good drink. Indeed on one return trip Bob was asked by customs how many bottles of brandy he had and Bob replied *'about four'* patting his tummy comfortably in front of the officer.

Comfortably because it was still there, the brandy, that is. On the homeward bound leg of that trip the captain had announced he planned to do a stalling exercise, quite an exciting operation in a huge Bristol Freighter, but Bob had missed the announcement. The shock and induced panic when the engines cut was something his mates didn't let him forget for weeks.

It was on one of these trips that Bob met Sylvie the Silver City air hostess. It is quite strange in view of the leg pulling that went on between these three companions that this alliteration did not beget more attention, I mean, 'Sylvie from Silver City' has fairly obvious attractions. It was the attractions of Sylvie that brought Bob and she together for an affair which ran and ran.

There are stark contrasts between the clinical smooth

perfumed ultra smart lifestyle of the female cabin crew of an airline and a farmer, even when he's been well scrubbed, the ruddy tan and hard hands don't come off. So what was the attraction? Well clearly the attraction to them both was the contrast, made plain to Bob when Sylvie later told him she was engaged to be married to another member of the airline stationed on their Glasgow Isle of Man run.

Obviously Bob wouldn't care at first. Like any man this was a new and attractive female who fancied him so who cares what her other attachments were. They went out together for nearly seven months and Bob was beginning to feel good about it save for the nagging thought that she was engaged. It could not therefore ever be permanent, was he, he would think, her wild oats? Her bit of rough?

Sylvie was living with her brother and parents at Ruckinge and it should be said, and their Alsatians, of which Bob was not considerably fond. Bob is on record of blaming those damn dogs for spoiling more than one evening of promised bliss.

Most of his courting was done in his old Ford popular which he lovingly called his courting car because the door handles were broken off on the inside. He would grin and say they can get in but not out, not in a hurry anyway. The affair came to an end, but not before Bob had rolled his beloved car over down the lane near Westview Hospital breaking Sylvie's little finger.[probably trying to get out.] So off she went back to the Glasgow operation of Silver City to marry, taking with her a memento, a broken finger; Bob would hope also some memories of her stay in Kent. The last he heard of Sylvie was a news flash that she was one of the survivors when a Silver City plane crashed in the mountains on the Isle of Man, one wonders if he might have thought that he at least only rolled his car over.

Evelyn was secretary of the Tenterden young farmers and it was impossible they weren't, if not thrown together, certainly sharing each other's company. Like the trip to Chatham Empire in 1957 where they shared a drink back stage with the, for the times, very riské comedian Max Miller. There was also' My Fair Lady' at Drury Lane on the winning of two tickets at Tenterden Young Farmers Club.

That didn't seem to trouble Bob in those days even although he later disliked the big City outings. Of course if you are with a young woman you fancy, it kind of waters down any aversions into nothing. If, you can organise a trip to Smithfield fat stock show with a variety show to follow, Bob with Evelyn, his girl in tow, then it mixed work with pleasure very nicely thank you. Even, even if the show title was the 'Love Birds' and the leg pulling was severe on the way home, it was all worth it

When children have grown up together, not exactly side by side but more or less on the same doorsteps, there may be a sort of, kissing cousin's familiarity, if you like, right through adolescence into manhood and womanhood respectively, then if they finally court one another and eventually marry it is impossible to say how long they courted. There are many such marriages, not slushy 'made in heaven' romances like in the novels. Marriages coming together like in nature where nothing could be more natural, where it surprises no one.

In the spring of ***1962***, as Evelyn her self puts it, *'I found myself pregnant'*. She doesn't say if it was a shock or if she was pleased, angry or scared, but Bob knew how he felt: Bob was apprehensive about what Evelyn's mother Gladys would say. Okay so it wasn't to be undone, it had to be faced, but keeping out of Glad's way couldn't go on forever. They agreed to tell Evelyn's mother on the Monday morning. The nearest Bob had been to Glad until then was when he'd been sent to mend a fence not a stones throw from their garden. Whilst he was working on it who should he see pacing too and fro in the garden but Evelyn's mother. The fence was finished in quick-sticks, if the old girl was so het up she was pacing the garden, what was Monday going to be like.

The confrontation was an anti climax. Bob had taken the initiative and said. *'Well Glad, are you going to give me a thick ear or take me down the pub and buy me a pint?'*

She bought him a pint.

What Bob only learned some time later was that the day he got all worried watching his future mother-in-law pacing up and down the garden was that she was actually planting seeds.

Their wedding was arranged for ***July 14th*** , strangely enough Bastille day, they had a slot for a civil ceremony at Ashford registry office and came back to the Vine Public House Tenterden for the reception. It hadn't escaped Bob's memory that his car might be in for a going over so he made sure that it was well hidden-up in a neighbour's garage at Goodshill, so they got away unscathed save for the usual confetti.

They had no destination in mind other than it would be the West Country. There first port of call was the Carpenters Arms at Mayfield to see Tom Griffiths and no doubt be reminded of the advice Bob was given months before on how to handle a new filly; *[Hold her head up high and kick her in the ribs]* then on to Yeovil to book in at the 'Three Choughs Hotel.'

At the Three Choughs their bedroom was commercial but pleasant enough, and country girl or no, Evelyn anticipated the sort of romantics most young women would, after all people don't have honeymoons all that often. Alright, she was two months pregnant and there were less secrets anymore but that still left lots of room for romance.

They had eaten well that evening and had a few drinks in the bar situated approximately under their room from where the distant hubbub of bar noise and street sounds was all there was to disturb them. Bob, ever incorrigible could not resist spoiling the romance for he immediately swooped under the covers loudly broke wind *[farted; for those with less easily offended sensibilities]* and threw the sheets over Evelyn's head.

Evelyn found strength from a mixture of anger and disappointment; she wasn't affronted, she knew her man better than that, nevertheless she pulled up her knees placed her feet firmly in her new husband's back and shoved him out of bed. Bob crashed onto the floor with such force it must have been heard in the bar below. *'It was a joke.'* he protested. *'They call it a Dutch Oven in these parts.'*

'Yes I'll bet they do' agreed Evelyn. *'And I just took the Jockey Club's advice and kicked you in the ribs, okay?'*

Next morning they continued on over Dartmoor into Cornwall over the Tamar Bridge and finally settled into the Salutation Arms at East Looe. Now East Looe has quite a little fishing industry going for it with trips out for the tourists and for the more serious deep sea sport or 'game fishing' as the Americans might call it. Bob very soon got to know the fishermen and was out fishing for Pilchards on the third night of his honeymoon.

But getting to know the fishermen wasn't just a turn of phrase, Bob had a real knack of knowing people and this was, in this case, helped by the two and half gallon flagon of very best 'Bob Luck' cider Bob never went anywhere without.

The river inlet between East and West Looe is tidal and when the water was up the only way across was to pay the ferryman and cross in a small dinghy which he would paddle standing up with one oar at the rear of the dinghy. At low water however the depth was such that dinghy need only be pushed across to keep the passengers, usually tourists, feet dry.

Somerset and Devon people know all about cider: Cider is that refreshing golden drink you take in pints, sweet or dry, you gulp it down over the back of the tongue, it has neither to be sipped like Sherry nor thrown over like spirit; yes Cider to these people is a *'long'* drink. It is logical to believe that these West Country fishermen might have said to one another. 'What can they know about Cider making in Kent?' they may even have joked. 'They'll be making Kentish Cream next' such may have been their attitude.

The ferrymen were introduced to Bob Luck Cider by Bob, as a sort of east west gesture of friendship, and they liked it, this was the man they'd fished with the night before and hadn't he boasted about this superior Cider he'd brought with him to the quay. Alas they underestimated the quality; they came back for more, drinking it like it was their own, only better tasting with a smooth liqueur consistency, not rough or sharp, indeed very good stuff.

Today they would have been charged with being drunk in charge of a dinghy, but in 1962 there were probably no charges that would fit the occasion. Not only were tourists tipped out of their dinghies into the shallow water but the ferrymen were misjudging the tide and ending up shoulder deep themselves in their efforts to fight the warm brain numbing effects of Bob Luck's 23% proof Cider.

To the incoherent cries of 'wine in um' East Looe would remember the shameful day the ferrymen couldn't hold their Cider.

The honeymoon came to an end all too soon as the weather was kind and the fishing good. Bob managed to fit in a bit of shark fishing and caught one just to prove that's where he'd been.

Soon they were back home in Tenterden to start married life with just a cooker downstairs and a bedroom up stairs with the picture of 'Pochard Rising' by Vernon Ward, a painting Evelyn had bought for Bob in the August and one where he'd told his father he didn't have to get out of bed to go shooting now; a remark Evelyn duly accepted as an endorsement of her gift. It wasn't the wish of every newly married young woman to live with one's in-laws. Evelyn remembers the light being switched on every morning at five thirty am. Father-in-law's idea of an early call system for young Bob, but taking away the little privacy they should have had.

The baby was due on the 31st Dec 1962 and that year was one of the worst winters on record with deep drifts and roads blocked for days. Everyone was worried lest Evelyn might not get to Kench Hill nursing home when the time arrived but Bob was unmoved saying he would get her there even if he had to drag her there himself on a piece of tin. But it didn't come to that and their new baby girl perhaps put off by the cold waited until the 7th January ***1963*** before weighing in at eight pounds 10oz. She was to be christened Ann.

1965 They moved into one of the new cottages built at Goodshill. This was a refreshing relief from the one room existence of living with the in-laws and at last laid the ghost of Evelyn's first week of married life and her Mother-in-laws kitchen. The strange orange stains on the walls and ceiling were, Bob told her, from his bachelor days when coming home one evening he'd decided to cook himself something to eat. Bob couldn't cook, not even an egg, but this attempt dated back to when he thought he might try. He had rummaged through his mother's store cupboard and found a tin of ravioli which he duly placed in a pan of water and lit the gas under it. Once again, if Bob had remembered his school days and the Charles Laws in particular, he would have remembered that that the pressure of gas varies with temperature and might just have made a hole in the tin. Alas he chased the dogs off the couch and settled down to wait for his ravioli to heat up. Of course he fell asleep in the process of waiting. Curled up on the couch with the terriers warm against his body he was far away in his dreams when the can exploded with a loud bang, followed by a mini Vesuvius spattering the walls and ceilings with hot indelible tomato coloured juice. Initially the dogs hid under the couch then when it was safe came out to taste the little runs of liquid off the kitchen walls. Bob was always to leave the cooking to the women after that.

Evelyn recalls that a washing machine would have been a godsend what with the baby and farm work being so dirty, she even found cow dung in his pockets, but young Bob always expressed the view wives and washing machines were synonymous; *'huh! I married one oh them things.'* He's on record as saying. Boilers and hand washing were common enough in the sixties still.

Evelyn was always a match for her joker husband but often let his little trick go without comment or retaliation. There was one day when she could not let things ride the way they had, for on this occasion she had got all smartened up in readiness to go out. She had put on a nice new 'T' shirt, crisp newly pressed blue jeans and best shoes, to say nothing of her hair and make up, the works, in other words. Before going out there was something she needed to talk to Bob about and she found him hosing down the cow shed with his thumb over the end of the hose for maximum pressure. On hearing her call out to him he turned on her with the hose and to his apparent glee hosed her down from head to toe.

This was not funny. Any epithets exchanged are not recorded but suffice to say Evelyn's first priority was to get dry and change her clothes. So it was in the fury of peeling off her wet clothes she plotted revenge and she knew Bob's Achilles heel alright.

Bob couldn't go very long without a drink and she knew he kept a quart bottle of cider underneath the seat of his old van which was parked beside the Oast. Waiting until Bob was occupied she stole into the van and took the cider bottle back to the house where she substituted the cider for a concoction of vinegar, curry powder and cayenne pepper and then returned it the its hiding place.

Evelyn knew that before very long Bob would need a quick swig of cider and sure enough she watched him go to the van and pull out the bottle, remove the stopper, put it to his mouth and throw back his head. The resulting gasp as the vinegar caught his breath and the sharp heat of the curry powder settled in his throat was a very satisfying revenge for Evelyn and although a hint of concern crossed her mind when he finally came up for air and smiled at her she knew the score was levelled.

The Sale of Heronden - 1977

In 1977 Evelyn's father Leo decided to sell Heronden to John Leroy the airline entrepreneur as the time was opportune, Evelyn's mother having passed away in March of that year and the strong memories associated with their life at Heronden being difficult for her father to cope with. Young Bob and Evelyn were both saddened as this had been their love and happy hunting ground [literally] for so many years. No more calling in the flights of duck on the Newmill levels, Riding out and lookering the sheep, those days were over. In the meantime old Bob had bought the 200acre property known as Crit Hall at Benenden and of course the area was familiar to them all, especially young Bob who's formative stamping ground it was. There were two cottages attached to, or more accurately, went with the property at Crit Hall along with the usual Barns, paddocks and interestingly, stock pens used by a previous owner Lord Vesty for rearing Bulls for exporting to the Argentine. Evelyn's father in law decided for some reason to allocate them the remoter South Cottage in Nineveh lane, possibly because he wanted his farm labourer Sid Bristol where he could see him. This left Evelyn rather isolated with the children and not being allowed to drive she was to some extent captive to the farm work of rearing calves, pigs, and rabbits; doing naturally what some 'Townie's' say they aspire to, 'self sufficiency'.

There is a long standing joke which in agricultural circles never raises quite so much eyebrow as when Townies and urban people tell it. This is perhaps because the funny part, or punch line, if you like, is often taken as make-believe.

It is the story of a couple of 'self sufficiency' types say of the ilk of Richard Briers and Felicity Kendal from that popular TV programme 'The Good life' who decided that their pet sow should be mated. The prospect of having a large litter of piglets was after all, a sort of *'bacon forever'* dream. They did the right thing and contacted their local farmer to see if that could be arranged thinking he would just bring his Boar round and let nature take its course. *'Oh no I am much too busy for that'* said the farmer *'and anyway the sow must always come to the Boar, you bring it round and there'll be no problem'*. The couple wondered how they would manage to get their huge pet sow down to the farm, they tried to herd her along, each with a stick, but despite their smacking and prodding she wouldn't go straight. They tied a rope around her neck and she went all stubborn like a donkey when they pulled at her. They'd heard the old wives tale that if you pull a pigs tail it will go forward but theirs just squealed. In the end the solution was to load their fat old pet into a wheel barrow then, with the greatest of difficulty, wheel the blessed pig down to the farm where at last the farmer's Boar covered the sow. But the story, funny as it was, didn't end there, because the farmer said that to be sure of results it would be best if the mating was repeated the next day. The idea of having to go through the trauma of catching and loading the sow the next morning was quite daunting for the couple and to add to their disquiet she was not in the sty when they went to look for her. They searched and searched until, just at the point of giving up, there she was; where else, but sat in the barrow.

Of course it is a fairy tale, a smutty story you might tell over dinner, a half truth about enjoyable sex if you like, but is it?

Young Bob loaded this, his first sow onto his lorry and ran her down the farmer at Bishopsden to get her covered. Now Bishopsden is a mile or two from Frogs Hole and pigs have poor eyesight so she couldn't have been making a note of the turnings, if you get my meaning, but when they discovered she was missing the day after being with the Boar she was found at, where else, Bishopsden. Of course it must be acknowledged that pigs have an excellent sense of smell, superior even to the best of hounds.

At Crit Hall one of old Bob's new ventures was the production of fertile eggs for turkey production which in the days before AID became common place, involved fitting the hen birds with leather saddles. Now for those who do not understand the physiology of birds and turkeys in particular, the system is approximately as follows. The birds ovaries produce a little chain of eggs, perhaps three to five at a time and these eggs pass into the equivalent of the birds womb where the stag's seamen has been deposited thus fertilizing the string of eggs. These eggs are laid over a period of three to seven days when, if you are in the business of fertile egg production, the hen bird should be put to the stag again.

So why the leather saddles? All the time the eggs are taken away from the hen bird she will continue to ovulate and lay her eggs; only if she is permitted to sit on a clutch of eggs will her hormones signal the cessation of egg production. To continue with the production of fertile eggs therefore decrees she be mated every four or so days. The hen turkey weighs on average 20lbs and the stag as much as 75lbs, not the best arrangement when it comes to the mating game, as the frequency for commercial egg production of this kind demands would have fatal results were the hen birds not protected from the stag's claws by the leather saddles. Unprotected sex was therefore dangerous for Turkeys too, until happily the development of AID made life easier if less fun, but as young Bob would have said, '*they get no sex but they still have Christmas to look forward to.*'

Life at South Cottage in Nineveh lane was remote indeed, certainly Evelyn had the two girls, but her immediate surroundings were her world.

It was what went on in the lane that provided changes to the daily routine of animal husbandry and not least of all was the very busy and widely renowned Riding Establishment at Great Nineveh run by Captain Kendal. A constant traffic of horses riding out with young riders under instruction down the many quiet lanes in and around Benenden was the norm. The Establishment had a first class cross country course of one and a half miles where eventers would come to compete. The time limit of less than ten minutes was held under the British Horse Society Rules. The establishment contributed to the local Gymkana and added considerably to the colour and excitement with a musical ride before the crowds at Benenden Fete in the summer.

It was, incidentally, at a similar fete, in the next village of Biddenden that a local man Peter Brown lived in a one hundred and forty gallon Bob Luck cider barrel for a week to raise funds for the church roof.

This man, peter Brown lived in a Bob Luck 140 gallon cider barrel for a week in aid of the church roof fund at Biddenden

With Evelyn's back ground and love of horses and young Bob's instinctive attraction to these animals their period at south Cottage was not without interest. They bought a black Shetland cross pony for the girls and easily melted into the equestrian atmosphere. Old Bob would on occasions wonder down from Crit Hall to see Evelyn, have a chat, steal from her vegetable garden and almost habitually steal any cakes if she'd been baking, but she tolerated her father in law, she knew his ways well by now. It was on one such visit he mourned the lack of a grandson, a Bob Luck the third if you like; wouldn't it be nice if? Granddaughters were lovely but in every man there is an innate dynasty streak; immortality through progeny, but Evelyn put him straight, bringing up the girls was hard enough and children don't come cheap.

If old Bob had asked the same question of his son, young Bob would have grinned and said. '*We got two lovely girls and we shan't have no more cos that old ford I drive would shake the balls off anything!*'

Did Evelyn wonder to herself, why when young Bob was so much in her father in law's own likeness he wasn't satisfied? Was her husband much like his father? Perhaps he didn't like what he saw, because young Bob was too much a reflection of himself. Was there not room for two practical jokers in the same dynasty? If she did wonder, she never got the answer.

Life at South Cottage wasn't without its spats. Old Bob had taken on the farm, a woman named S****, she was a farm hand; and an ex land-girl. Charlie Savage then a young teenager also employed by old Bob remembers her as good to work for. Evelyn only came in contact with her when the woman wanted help. She had a horse she could barely manage and Evelyn helped straighten it, and her out, when she brought it down to South Cottage, they got on not too badly and up to a point she found her amiable enough. S**** had confided in her about the last farm she worked on where she had stepped through some rotten floor boards and sued for compensation. She recounted happily that she got £20,000 from the old man, adding you've got to get what you can out of these old bugger's. Taken in passing conversation woman to woman Evelyn took it as small talk, but later events were to prove otherwise. The two girls, Julie and Ann sensed something about S**** in a way that only children do. They were wary of her and seemed to share a private opinion in a way young people do, between them they christened her 'baggy pants'. Physically S**** was not a small woman, indeed she was a rather masculine woman, and neither Michael nor young Bob found her easy to know. Young Bob who could get on with nearly anybody, knew there was definitely something about her he couldn't place. He nick-named her Twiggy.

Old Bob was it seems besotted with S****. She had appeared at Crit Hall as if by magic, as though she had been there all the time. She had an influence on old Bob rather like a female Rasputin would have, influencing his deliberations about the farm. It wasn't long before this chemistry of unease manifested itself into trouble.

Young Bob and S**** crossed swords in the yard at Crit Hall, where they were unloading lump wood. Something was said which in the passage of time has been lost but whatever it was young Bob took offence and called her a bloody bitch. Now young Bob was an amiable man who even when he maligned someone lent always a glimmer of humour to his words. To days words however seemed to carry no such insurance for S**** stepped forward and knocked him down with a right hand worthy of a prize fighter. Young Bob who was tough and was knocked down by shock more than impact, got to his feet dusted himself down and repeated *'You bloody bitch!'* his words this time fuelled by a combination of venom and the embarrassment of being knocked over by a woman.

No sooner had the words left his lips than she swiped him again, flooring him a second time. Any gentlemen that may have lurked within young Bob's character was gone, now his blood was up and all the strength of a young farmer with it. He quickly rose to his feet and smacked the woman he called Twiggy really hard. She toppled over backwards, crashing onto her back hitting her head and splitting it open on the concrete.

Soon we had a confrontation between old Bob and his

son. A terrible division of loyalties for old Bob the besotted old man who now must choose to support either his eldest son or his lover. What was to be done about this assault? Young Bob knew that anyone witnessing such an incident would understand and shrug it off, after all what was a bump on the head compared with the indignity he had suffered. But he counted without knowing the feelings his father had for the woman S****.

Old Bob turned on Evelyn, looking she supposed for the woman's angle, the sympathy a woman might have for another woman knocked down by a man. *'What are you going to do about it? He ranted'.* Evelyn wanted to say she had it coming but a sort of neutrality prevailed and the confrontation dissipated. She too thought the problem would go away on its own.

The next day the police called at Wealden Heights, where they now lived. Bob was shocked to see them, it was only a bump on the head after all, and he'd been floored twice and had the indignity of telling the policemen that. Mostly the thought that his father had rounded on him in that way, and had not kept it in the family hurt him. A statement was taken and he was charged with 'Actual Bodily harm.' His father and his lady friend had alleged he had struck her over the head with a piece of wood which they actually produced as evidence in court at Cranbrook where on the 6th march 1972 Young Bob was fined £25 and bound over to keep the peace for two years.

In the seventies whist living at Wealden Heights Bob had a run in with one of his neighbours living at West Winds. The neighbour was Colonel Wynn-Jones retired and to say it was a run in might be an exaggeration for as far as Bob was concerned it was just an exchange of words. Bob was out with his gun looking for a rabbit, for rabbits had come full cycle and as everyone had predicted had bounced back from the horrible disease inflicted on them in the fifties.

The rabbit Bob shot was a good spread shot to his right, say thirty yards, whilst behind him over his left shoulder was the garden of West Winds, and in the garden the gallant Colonel doing what retired people do in their gardens. Clearly the shot had startled the Colonel for he shouts, nay bellows, across the space between him and Bob. *'Hey you my man! You almost shot me!'*

Bob couldn't believe his ears. *'There lies the rabbit over there.'* He said pointing at the now still grey form in the grass.

'I shall tell your father about this, I know when I've been shot at, I am a professional soldier you know.'

This, thought Bob was ridiculous, he still hadn't picked up the rabbit, there it was in a totally different direction. *'A professional are you? I've heard about your lot, they issued you all with Ox guns didn't they? So's you could shoot bloody bull shit!'*

The Colonel did tell Bob's father but got no change from his complaint. Young Bob would shrug his shoulders as it was no big deal, saying. *'Rats can't breed Mice and Rooks don't breed Jack-daws.'* Life wasn't that complicated.

The Crit Hall Fire Brigade

Old Bob was very fond of a good fire and many rural houses right up to the sixties in this part of Kent if not the south of England had large fireplaces ranging from Inglenook's big enough to walk into, through medium Bessemer beamed types right down to *yer actual* brick cottage York stone hearthed models.

Old Bob's home was no exception with new sawn logs of apple cord-wood stacked neatly *[or haphazardly by Bob, Evelyn relates]* either side of the hearth. The ambience created by the sweet smell of apple wood was homely and very much part of the Kent rural scene.

The oft heard joke about being short on sawyers and too lazy to wield an axe was not so far fetched for on one occasion when ready cut wood was short Bob had fed the dry end of a hop pole into the fire leaving the rest to be stepped over, hitching it further into the fire as it burned. Of course we're meant to imagine the twenty foot pole going out though the kitchen window, funny as that thought is, but doubtless logs were allowed to lay on the hearth to be kicked further in as they burned down.

Withstanding the ravages of a good fire years on end had brought the repair and rebuilding of the fireplace in old Bob's house at Crit Hall well into the realms of urgent and, after such a repair he was told not to light a fire as the job was not complete. Seeing no obvious reason for such compliance Bob went ahead and lit a fire not knowing that part of the job included some electrical work.

Of course the inevitable happened, the insulation melted and the resulting short circuit set alight to the lathe and plaster walls on the ground floor. Realising he couldn't put out the blaze himself, old Bob went to phone the Brigade but not before he'd dashed upstairs to where his wife lay in bed, calmly reassuring her the house was on fire but not to worry as he was just off the get the Fire Brigade.

The premise that lightning doesn't strike the same place twice was confounded by a second fire within a fortnight. Too embarrassed to telephone the Brigade once more and no doubt openly owning up to the responsibility he shouted about the farm for Sid Bristol.

Now Sid was a sort of *'man about the farm'* in old Bob's employ and one of Sid's functions was to see that the chicken and rest of the stock got well watered. To make this chore less onerous Sid had designed a contraption in the form of a water bowser which was simply a large cylinder supported on two wheels, no more than a ten gallon drum but nevertheless a labour saving initiative.

When old Bob revealed the house was on fire, again, Sid, no doubt laughing through his teeth, galloped off the get his water bowser and eventually the pair of them managed to put out the fire.

From that day on, anywhere about the farm, Sid and his contraption were referred to as the Crit Hall fire brigade.

When the young Charlie Savage started work for old Bob at Crit Hall he was just a teenager about eighteen. The reputation of his employer had not yet reached the young mans ears and of course eager to please he was up for any sort of work, be it on the farm or at the cider works. One day old Bob asked him to go to the work shop and bring him back an adjustable spanner. Now the workshop was separated from the main work space by a sliding door and young Charlie noticed that as he reached the door old Bob was still behind him. Of course he was thinking why was the old man behind him? Why if he had come along as well, couldn't he get the spanner himself? Was this some sort of test? Like in the army when they send you to the stores for a rubber hammer. Conscious of the old man behind him he took hold of the handle and jerked the door aside, where to his horror standing upright in the shadows was a coffin and the staring eyes of a corpse.

The shock was immense and some minutes elapsed before the lad realised this was a dummy in the coffin. He turned to see the old man laughing at him and strained to see the funny side of it himself. From that day on Charlie was to be wary of old Bob and his jokes. Evelyn recounts that the coffin was bought at a sale and the dummy was a tailor's shop dummy made up to be very death-like. The coffin featured more than once, and the dummy appeared in the beds of any local person not prudent enough to keep their doors locked; on one occasion one local lady returned home to find someone sat on her toilet, initially tempted to shut the door and proffer her apologies before realising it was a dummy sat there knees akimbo. Such was the trouble old Bob would go to for a laugh. The amazing psychology of this man who after all would not sometimes see the effects of his japes, for, not being present, would have to imagine what shock or discomfort or frivolity they might generate.

Drink Driving Ban - Dec 14th 1968

One thing is certain, if young Bob had still lived at Goodshill farm he wouldn't have been stopped by the Police at Rolvenden Station on the 14th December 1968, but alas he was on his way home to Benenden and there they were with their *'Good evening Sir'* formality, politely asking him to blow gently into this. He was duly charged with driving a motor vehicle having consumed alcohol in excess of the legally permitted limits. Young Bob appeared at the Tenterden Petty Sessions Court held, strangely, at Cranbrook where he pleaded guilty and was fined £25 with 10 guineas costs and disqualified from driving for twelve months.

Bob's attitude was that if he got caught, then he got caught, and he was resigned to take what the law decreed, so resigned indeed that he borrowed a bike to ride the three miles to Cranbrook for the court case. Bicycles and Bob were not very compatible indeed after running out road a few times he was to abandon them for a while as a mode of transport complaining that *'pedalling like stink just to give yer arse a ride'* wasn't his idea of motivation. For his years sabbatical from driving he was always able to persuade a friend to chauffeur him when needed.

Breathalysed Again April - 1971

Young Bob got his licence back in 1970 and sold some shares he had in Decca Electrical to buy himself a brand new Ford Escort Van. Evelyn also passed her driving licence in November of the same year having been prohibited from driving because of her childhood epilepsy. Suddenly they were both mobile. Then Bob was pulled over by the police patrol in Small Hythe Road not far from the William Caxton Ph. He had been on his way to Rye to look at a boat with a view to sea fishing but alas it was never to come about. Evelyn got a message from Ashford police station to say he was there and of course she had to fetch him home, not the easiest of tasks as the police had locked up the van and taken the keys to Ashford.

This time, it not being long after the return of his licence, Bob was already thinking about learning to ride that damned bike again. The police had apprehended him and the police surgeon had duly taken and supplied him with his own blood sample as is the law. The samples are enclosed in a small phial with a seal through which the needle injects the blood. The phials already contain enough anti coagulant to ensure against deterioration. The case held again at Cranbrook on the 13/04/71 proved to be complex in as much as the analysts could not test the blood sample. The anticoagulant had not preserved the blood sample as it was supposed to do and therefore the analysts could not determine its alcohol content with sufficient accuracy required by law.

Instead of simplifying the case this complication only served to prolong it even although the outcome was clearly going to favour young Bob. The court had to hear the County analyst, the police analyst and the private analysts submissions before finding the case dismissed. The grounds for dismissal were that Bob had not been supplied with a blood sample suitable enough for analysis. The case had taken from 10am until 5pmn to resolve. Of course Bob had his Solicitors fees and analyst's fees [£60] to pay but breathed a sigh of relief at the end of it. He was so elated he made the mistake of commenting *[too gleefully perhaps cheekily, words we shall never know]* to the constable on the case when he might really have been better to bite his tongue.

The Move to Millpond Farm - 1973

The move to Millpond farm from Wealden Heights on the 24th Jan 1973 wasn't so much a bolt for freedom from the apron strings of old Bob after being so long living in his shadow; but a sort of imposed independence.

The move certainly had its problems and it is a credit to young Bob and Evelyn that they were able to build up their newly acquired small farm so quickly from such small beginnings. They arrived at the sixty five acres Millpond farm with five calves and one pig. There was a selection of concrete buildings in the form of a cow shed and some sty's but all needed considerable work and modification.

They had been offered the swill from Benenden Girls School and the opportunity was too good to be missed, this was followed by the Benenden Hospital Swill and some of the local pubs; a massive, though to some, obnoxious, potential for feeding pigs.

The regulations for feeding swill to pigs were, then as they are today, quite tight. The farm had no electricity, all the water had to be boiled using bottled gas. This was a big step back for Evelyn in particular, as with two children to bring up, clothes to be boiled and pressed using a gas iron may sound reasonably acceptable until you consider the implications of the ministry regulations on the preparation of pig swill. The overalls, clothes, and utensils used in the handling of the uncooked swill should never be allowed to come in contact with the overalls and etc. used for the prepared feed, indeed the two areas even the buildings were kept separate too. To a farmer's wife, and not forgetting in the case of Evelyn, she was a farmer too, not just a house keeper and mother, keeping clothes clean and dry was the most perennial and enduring chore.

Precaution against swine fever was the reason for these regulations. To make the point, not too long ago a northern Pig Breeder was suspected as being the probable cause of the UK's last Foot and Mouth disease out-break by the very reason of contaminated swill. Young Bob and Evelyn modified their buildings and followed the regulations. Soon they had nearly a hundred store pigs; a very large expansion and amount of work.

Both young Bob and Evelyn had unpleasant experiences with the swill which only become funny when told after time. They used to pick up the drums of swill and load them into the back of their Sherpa van and providing they were driven carefully that was okay. On one occasion Evelyn had to swerve to avoid another car then stop suddenly. The drums slid forward hit the back of the seats drenching her with the swill. As she says there were custard, apple pudding and beans running down her face that day.

For a small farm the activities were various and labour intensive. As well as rearing pigs they coppiced their woodland and sold it off to Bowaters Mills Sittingbourne for pulping in the manufacture of paper, an added means of revenue. This was a common woodland activity in Kent usually on an eight year cycle. Depending on the wood species, sometimes chestnut was sold for fencing posts and spiles. They also acquired some sheep which immediately gave them problems as the breed were Welsh Mountain Sheep and their farm boundaries were three strand post and wire fences. Bob would complain that the little Welsh b****s were high calibre escape artists; indeed he named one of them, a little black one more like a goat then a sheep, Alfie Hinds after the convict who was forever escaping from prison.

All the boundary fencing had to be renewed because of their acquired flock by the addition of sheep netting which hints obliquely at the lack of forward planning, but in subsistence farming, as this was and always is when just setting up, the opportunities have to be grasped when they are offered and the problems solved in arrears. From the small one pig and five calves beginning, to upwards of a hundred pigs, calves, sheep, chicken and two children; it is easy to see a massive amount of work.

Usually when flu strikes it hits one partner then the other so that the recovering victim can nurse the suffering victim, but this particularly virulent flu hit Bob and Evelyn at the same time. No way could either rise from their beds save to feed the children, and with mother in laws help send them off to school. But what about the stock?

Their recent coppicing had brought them into contact with Nigel Kemp who was working woodland near to theirs at Children's farm. They had become good friends and when Nigel heard of their plight he filled the breach, turning out each day to feed and water the stock until they were on their feet again. Such neighbourliness in small farming circles often surprises the uninformed simply because the neighbour isn't over the fence, next door, or across the road, but often separated by miles of fields and not seen on a daily basis.

Nigel was a good neighbour and a real friend to Bob who's impish use of words labelled him 'Nidge,' 'The Viking' or 'Jesus' because of his mop of unruly fair hair and blonde beard; fuelled perhaps by a little of the green eye as Bob's hair was already thinning.

Some friendships are instant but most develop over time when the knowledge and character of the individuals concerned gels with a chemistry understood by no one. With Nigel and Bob the friendship was one of the instant sort.

Nigel was a joker too. No, he wouldn't go out of his way to do anything flamboyant, he would never have put a dead fox in the back of someone's car, nothing like that; he would just seize an opportunity when it was offered.

Bob and he were working in a wood, coppicing together. Whether it was Chestnut for spiles, Birch for brush heads or just wood for pulp they were for once working side by side in a wood owned by a local rather formidable old lady by the name of Miss Ardley who then lived at Whitelands farm near Silcocks Farm. Now Miss Ardley was one of three landowning ladies known rather unkindly as the three witches. Undeserved as this title was this diminutive old lady with a strong crusty voice, and false leg, who went shopping in the village of St Michaels with an old donkey and two dogs was indeed formidable; a rare woman that even young Bob wouldn't stand up to willingly.

The standing timber had been bought from Miss Ardley

by Bob on the condition that the three or four substantial oak trees were left standing. Now it happened that one of these oaks was badly damaged during the work and there was nothing else they could do but fell it. It was the right thing to do; no self respecting woodsman would leave a badly skinned tree like that, it was rather like putting a wounded pheasant out of its misery.

Bob thought no more about it, he was concerned, but it was done now. The time came for him and Evelyn to go and get the pig swill and when they got back to Nigel his face was ashen.

'Wot's up with you then Nidge?' Bob asked.

Nigel shook his head from side to side seriously. *'Miss has been down, wants to know wot's appened to her tiller? Ses there were four and now there's only three.'*

'Oh bugger! She aint has she?' By now Bob was doing mental arithmetic, oak wasn't cheap. *'How many cube do you reckon was in that tree then Nidge?'*

Nigel looked up at the clouds as though the answer was written up there, then pretended to count on his fingers.

At this point Bob detected a twinkle behind the eyes of his friend. *'You old sod you're aving me on! She aint been down here at all.'*

The furthest Nigel ever went with a joke was at the hop picking for Gerald Orpin at New Barn farm. They were quite a happy crew of workers, they'd all known each other a long time and leg pulling was a way of life. Nigel was working in the crows nest, a sort of gantry pulled behind a tractor, his job was to cut the bines at wire level, whilst at the bottom Charlie Roberts, was cutting the bines at the banding in point. Now this involves a sort of stop start process as far as the tractor driver is concerned; Richard Hukins Bob's cousin was one of the drivers. If the crows nest man wasn't quick he could be left dangling from the wire or the bines didn't get cut. Anyway, not just one but all the drivers this day had been making life difficult for Nigel and he swore mentally he'd get his own back.

One evening after work Nigel tapped Evelyn for a few eggs, not just good ordinary eggs but five or six addled goose eggs. Arriving before the tractor drivers next day he slipped a couple eggs under the old hessian sacking on the steel sprung seats of each tractor and went about his business. Of course farm workers never mount their tractors gently, do they? The seats are nice springy things same shape '*as yer bum*' so to speak. On this site such was the rivalry to get to the hop gardens first, getting onto the tractors was more of a Le Mans start, the drivers arrived, started up and plonked! themselves down with a crunch, a squelch, and a smell, that was to live with him all day.

Nigel had a vehicle called a Mini Moke. It was a sort of cut down mini made by the Austin motor corp; or whatever their title was at that time. It was the type of vehicle more at home on the sand dunes of Spain hired out to tourists, khaki or olive green in colour, it had no doors and a canvass tilt, quite military in flavour really.

Nigel kept his, full of all the wood cutter's tools of the trade like chain saws and ropes, stuff like that. With the tilt taken off this vehicle was ideal for shooting at night and Bob and he and Evelyn would pile into it with Bob leaning over the top of the screen with his gun and Evelyn operating the lamp.

Along the top of the screen bar were a number of raised press studs to which the tilt could be fastened and these were the only undesirable thing about the whole facility as later after a night of jostling about the fields resting his chest against the screen bar Bob was heard to exclaim. *'Look at this Mister Kemp that bloody Moke thing o' yorn as near ripped my tits orf.'* Needles to say they were often reduced to fits of laughter being bounced about the country in Nigel Kemps Mini Moke.

One day Bob had expressed to Evelyn his desire to go fishing off Dungeness for Cod which under most circumstances she would have gladly agreed to, being now the only one allowed to drive. But, the snag was it was a night fishing trip and Evelyn drew the line at driving him down to the coast for a two am. start with the probability of having to return for him the next day. It was at this point Nigel stepped into the breach and said he would deliver him and his fishing gear to the beach in time for the off.

That was fine but Bob had forgotten his sustaining flagon

of cider, a must on any fishing trip. It was Nigel who provided him with a bottle of his mother's Elderflower wine thinking, quite reasonably, that would do him no harm.

When Evelyn went out to Dungeness the next day to collect him twelve hours later he was, at first, nowhere to be seen, just his fishing gear laid at the side of the road. She eventually spotted him coming down the road weaving to and fro like, as Bob was later to describe *'Like a postman with business both sides of the street.'* Once inside the passenger seat of the van he collapsed over the gear stick, his hands and arms flaying about such that the lights went on, the wipers were going on and off and the dogs were fussing over him licking his face and generally making life dangerous.

Evelyn pulled in at the petrol station at Lydd where she knew the owners and was immediately greeted with. *'Hello Evelyn got Bob with you?'*

'Open the van door and have a look.' she replied. There was Bob in a crumpled heap half in the foot well of the passenger side, half draped over the gear stick. *'You'll have to help me get him in the back where it's safer.'* She said. So with some help and no resistance save for his dead weight Bob was unceremoniously dumped in the back of the van on top of two sacks of shavings and with his dogs for company.

It was something like half three in the afternoon when they got home and no way could Evelyn either rouse him or shift him. At eight pm. that evening one of his mates came to see if Bob wanted to, of all things, go fishing, and it was he who managed to rouse Bob after his marathon sleep. Some time afterwards Bob recalled that as well as the Elderflower wine he had drunk a bottle of Saki rice wine which explained the stupor of the occasion and a state too delicate to accept the offer of another fishing trip just yet.

Breathalysed Again April - 1973

This time the police who had been following Bob from Tenterden took their last chance to overtake him in Grange road right next to Silcocks farm. After that point the road is so narrow Bob would have got away with it. Once again he was breathalysed and failed. This time Bob knew they might throw the book at him and was already mentally oiling his bike. He was found to be over the limit; found guilty and fined £25 plus £7:20 doctors fees, but worst of all he was banned from driving for three years.

The Demise of Old Bob - Feb 8th 1978

February the 3rd was Evelyn's birthday and just as young Bob had gone pilchard fishing off the Devon coast on his honeymoon so it must have seemed quite appropriate for him to go fishing off Dungeness with his mates on his wife's birthday. After all, these birthdays are worth celebrating and as has been related already, that was the day he fell over board only to be rescued by Alan King hooking him by the hood of his duffle smock . The aftermath of this episode had attracted the press and there was a lot of ribald banter around the issue of what exactly the Kent papers might say of the rescue. There was a certain irony about rescuing your mate on his wife's birthday; especially when later looking for praise you are politely told you should have thrown him back. Alan King's heroism seen through the eyes of a fishing-widow took some of the shine off his armour but there were still hopes of a bit of a laugh from the papers. Young Bob would probably have shrugged off the incident, commenting perhaps, that getting in there after them was after all the only way to fish. Alas the prospective excitement of a good press story was not to be, for five days later on February the 8th Bob's mother Freda telephoned to say that her husband old Bob had passed away.

Of course this was a big shock to them all. Old Bob was well liked not just in the family but around the county, in the markets, sale rooms and farms. For young Bob the death of his father must have been doubly shocking. Although they had fought and argued as fathers and sons the world over he was in his father's image sensitive and fun loving; more than anything possessed of a keen sense of justice. Young Bob he was no longer. Now he was Bob Luck.

In the mining villages up and down the country there used to be an unwritten rule that a miner never went down the pit if he had an unresolved matter with a loved one. The reason for this was that should he be trapped or killed or never come back there would be an extra burden of unresolved guilt resting upon the survivor.

Bob had had the big 'bust up' down at Crit Hall when he called his father's mistress a 'bloody bitch', things were never right after that, indeed that incident precipitated their move away from Wealden heights to St Michaels and Millpond farm. He'd been the black sheep, and black sheep often carry a burden not always of their own making.

Old Bob was dead. His widow Freda had known he was unwell when he came in that evening. She made him a drink and left him to go to bed. Next morning he was still sitting in the same chair. He had died in his sleep.

Evelyn says old Bob's Will was the beginning of a nightmare and although it is neither appropriate nor useful to divulge all the machinations of it, it will help us to view cursorily what old Bob had intended.

We know old Bob had approached Evelyn some few years before at South Cottage with the persuasive opinion that it would be nice to have another grandson, and how Evelyn had sent her father in law away with a flea in his ear and a lecture on the cost of bringing up children.

This desire somewhat sets the seal on old Bob's thinking as a man with a dynasty on his mind, a man who would like to see above all things the Luck family prosper and progress. Old Bob was a good business man he knew the potential and most of all he knew, for good or ill, the potential of his two sons young Bob and Michael.

When the will was read neither of his sons received a penny and out of his four grandchildren Ann, Julie, Richard and Fay it was his only grandson Richard who was the major beneficiary receiving Frogs Hole farm, business, and two cottages. This tells us as much as we may wish to read into it, but on the surface the manner of the allocations: Frogs Hole [The Cider works] was to be kept. *[in essence perpetuating the Luck name]* and Crit Hall was to be sold. Shares went to the three grand daughters and of course the bulk of his estate passed on to his widow Freda.

Rightly, it is hard for anyone to be resentful when money you expected to receive is given to your children. Whether old Bob's actions had a distinct message it may be ungracious to consider. A bitter man might say there was a meaning hidden in his father's allocations particularly as the macho Ms S**** received shares to the value of £18,000. Considerably more than his grand daughters received; but Young Bob was not a bitter man, he was not a man to bear a grudge and got on with his daily life as much as his father's plans for them permitted.

His father had reasoned than young Bob and his brother Michael would continue to run the Cider works at Frogs Hole. It was after all an already famous and established business, now, since his death, owned by his grandson Richard. Obviously when shaping his will he ignored the knowledge that his sons were very different and didn't always see eye to eye. To install them in the same arena to make their livelihood, side by side, showed he either didn't know them as well as he should, or this was his last little bit of devilment, his last big joke, his last fox in a barrel, to put his sons together.

Clearly no one would believe that. Clearly he hoped to see Bob Luck Cider progress, and his family with it; but it was not to be. By now young Bob and Evelyn were established at Millpond farm and things were going well. They had bought the land from Bob Luck Ltd., in return for young Bob's shares and felt independent; they resisted the changes the will seemed to demand. Likewise Michael was happy farming at Crit Hall and so the whole grand plan of their famous father was set into turmoil.

The trustees decided that the alternative was for Frogs Hole to be sold as neither Bob nor Michaels wanted to work it. This was duly done and Evelyn relates that never an apple was pressed after that day. At that time the provisions and regulations of the factories act were updated and it is clear that there would have been a large amount of capital needed to update the equipment there. Included in the transfer as assets of the business were two vats of liquer cider, four hundred gallons or so. The alcohol content of this cider was in the order of 30 proof and attracted the attention of Customs and Excise. Unable to pay the duty the new owners were forced to standby as the Excise Officers opened the taps and let this magnificent golden fluid drain away into the water course.

This Evelyn says was sacrilege. More symbolic however, this was the last life blood of a renowned cider maker, old Bob Luck, the joker, entrepreneur, a man with all the weaknesses of men and immortal through his son Young Bob.

Breathalysed Again April - 1980

Bob had regained his licence in 1976 and was soon on the road in about the lanes around Millpond Farm. Surprisingly Bob noticed he was attracting police vans like bees around a honey pot. He'd hardly go five miles without noticing one and even spotted one at the end of the lane. This of course kept young Bob on is toes but it soon began to irritate him.

A friend asked Bob one day how he was getting on now that he was driving gain, more a sort of pleasantry than a serious question to which Bob answered. *'Oh I shan't get in to trouble no more as I got a police escort everywhere, Just like bloomin royalty!'* It transpired that the friend had influence in police circles and the harassment stopped as if by magic.

Bob had been fishing down at Dungeness; April was a good month for mackerel and he was on his way home in the old Sherpa van; he'd got as far as Reading Street when he was stopped and breathalysed. Although cider production had ceased when old Bob died there was always a few two gallon flagons to be found. At least young Bob could find them, and naturally he took one fishing.

It was September before they were informed when the case was to be heard and at the time they were Hop Picking for Gerald Orpin who they had worked for spasmodically since 1972 after the incident with his old Bob's mistress S****. Neither Evelyn nor Bob worked for old Bob again full time after that year, young Bob working for his friend Jim Goodsell and Evelyn, hop tying, dressing and training for Gerald Orpin.

Old Bob did 'come round' eventually, and ask Bob and Evelyn if they would help out with the cider making, which they did right up until old Bob's death.

When Bob got his notice to attend the court in Ashford Evelyn told him she just could not go through all that again, to sit through another court case was a little more than she could put up with particularly as at his briefing with his solicitor he'd been warned that he must expect to go to prison. Alan King his long standing friend, volunteered to take him up to Ashford both knowing it could well be a single journey for Bob.

The Court was told Bob was three times over the legal limit of alcohol. The magistrate said it was the worst case of drink driving he'd ever heard. Leaning across the bench, holding Bob's stare, the judge told him he sentenced him to six months in prison, then he paused, interminably it seemed, although actually only for a few seconds, looked around the court and added, suspended for six months. Bob said afterwards that if the judge had wanted to put the wind up him then he had succeeded in those few seconds. But the judge hadn't finished. There was to be a massive £200 fine and a five year suspension followed by a Ministry driving test.

As Evelyn relates this was the very last straw for Bob's driving as he wouldn't have been able to handle the Ministry test with all the written work it entailed. So it was to be she who did the driving from then on.

What with going off to work for Gerald Orpin, driving Bob around to his work and various enterprises, looking after their own stock and fowl, days were often too short to get things done. It was as well the demands on the terriers had diminished due to Bob's incapacity but nevertheless they had their problems with litters of puppies, the dreaded parvo virus, and a cross mating by Jack a visiting collie from the nearby Honour Farm.

It was about December 1981. Dodger's litter of four dog pups were a month old and Evelyn was in the kitchen drawing some poultry when the bitch asked to go out. Some short while later she heard a yelp and immediately remembered Bob had set a fox wire in the hedge at the bottom of the garden. She went down to the hedge and there was Dodger in the fox wire. The wire was of the type designed to draw up tight something on the principle of a ratchet or if you like one of those plastic ties they use on electrical work nowadays. Anyway there was Dodger hardly breathing, her nose going blue and her eyes already bulging. Evelyn had been quick thinking enough to take with her some pliers but the wire was too tough. She admits she was panicking as she struggled to free her beloved servant. She shouted for Bob to come and help but to no avail. Mentally taking hold of herself she spared a second to stand back, telling herself '*come on Evelyn you can do this, you know how these thing work!*' Discarding the pliers she took hold of the wire and patiently started to thread it back through the eyelet a notch at a time until she had enough slack to release the dog. To her relief the near lifeless Dodger came round after some vigorous massaging, kind tearful words and emotional cuddles.

What that incident did for the local Fox population is difficult to assess but Evelyn gave Bob instructions he wasn't to set any more fox wires at Millpond Farm.

Ann and Julie

Bob and Evelyn had two daughters Ann and Julie separated by just sixteen months and as they grew so they were often taken for twins. Most men dote on their daughters and Bob was no exception, unlike his father's preoccupation with the dynasty, girls were good enough for him and he and Evelyn saw to it they wanted for very little.

When the children were of school age they went to Benenden School, the very same school that the then young Bob had attended all those years before. Bob and Evelyn were still living at Wealden Heights at that time but their move to Millpond Farm was to take Ann and Julie to St Michaels Village school aged ten and eight respectively. They were just two bubbly little country girls happy to go to school. They enjoyed, one guesses, with a little encouragement from their mother, herself a proficient horsewoman, going to the local pony club. Gymkhanas, Show jumping, Cross Country, and later Hunting with the Ashford valley Fox Hounds. Out hunting, on more than one occasion when the field had baulked at a hedge or fence one or other of the Hunt masters Johnny Hooker or Tom Betts would be heard to call out. *'Stand back and let those Luck girls show how it should be done.'* And Ann and her sister would take the fence in style and the whole field stream over after them.

At that time they had two strawberry roan ponies, one each. Ann rode an Arab cross Welsh gelding called Squirrel Nutkin nick-named Nutty for short. Julie had a New Forest type pony 13.2 hands high, same size as Ann's, called High Jinks and Jinks for short, well named as he was always messing around.

The sisters rode and looked after these ponies for about four years, Julie having had Jinks from the age of nine.

They both left school at sixteen, Ann being the eldest left first and found a job at Duckhurst Farm Staplehurst working for Ollie Jones. Naturally the job was around

Ann on Squirrel Nutkin

Julie hunting on Jinks

horses, schooling, training, riding out and bringing on youngsters. They also ran a riding school and went out show jumping at such places as Harwood Hall in Essex. Ann was jumping in classes with prestigious riders such as Marion Mould Née Marion Coates who had an Olympic horse called Stroller at that time before going on to marry David Mould who was the royal jockey for a period. Ann could hold her own against many experienced riders; she held all the pony club certificates for her age and was looking forward to her eighteenth birthday so she could step up a class.

Julie in the meantime had left school. Like her elder sister she too took on a stable job but was unable to get on with the people and left after three days. It was to be some months before she found a job to her liking, eventually working for Margaret Hooker at Harbourne farm. There she stayed for several years happily breaking horses, riding and show jumping, winning frequently with Margaret's horses and with her own. Young Bob and Evelyn had every right to feel proud of their two very successful young ladies.

Julie on Spook

Monday May 18th 1981

Ann had at the start of her job got herself a Yamaha Fsie motor cycle. It was after all the only means of getting herself to her work at Staplehurst each day as there was no public transport. Although technically a learner she was a very competent rider and had recently upgraded her machine. She left home that morning about half past eight.

Young Bob had decided they needed some new calves and he and Evelyn had loaded up their Sherpa van with logs the evening before meaning to deliver the logs then go off to the market at Maidstone. It is significant their route would have been the same as Ann's had they not had the logs to deliver in Benenden first. As it was their route cut out the section of road between Biddenden and Sissinghurst.

Bob and Evelyn had not been at Maidstone market long before she was approached by the auctioneer. He asked if she had Bob with her as at that moment Bob had gone off either to the loo or been caught up in conversation. '*Yes he's here somewhere, why?*' she asked. The auctioneer's manner was distant as though there was some obscure sense of seriousness in the message he had to impart.

'Its Michael, he's been the on the telephone and the message is you've to go home at once.'

Immediately Evelyn thought this was a leg pull. The auctioneer's straight face and the fact that this market, Maidstone, was reckoned between them to be Michael's patch for buying calves. For years Bob and Evelyn had used Ashford market for the very reason of not being in competition with family. Still of this opinion Evelyn asked to use the telephone and spoke to Michael who would not disclose the reason over the line as to why they must return. She went round the market and found Bob who after some thought said '*Well, we must go home then.*' He, the master joker, in his father's playground, where as a boy he'd watched his Dad empty peas down his fellow farmers Wellington; didn't think Michael was joking.

On crossing the market to their van they were approached by two police constables who asked were they Bob and Evelyn Luck, to which they replied affirmatively. '*Then you have to go straight home*' they said.

The police officers could not tell them why. Evelyn had by now a distinct feeling of foreboding something, she knew, was seriously wrong, but what? Was it the girls, were they alright?

In the thirties no one ever got a telegram without it being bad news. In the fifties it was a constable at the door and now in modern times it's a police officer or more likely two and police car. This is how it is, no one has to tell you what it is about, except that it is serious; a knowledge that exists in the sub conscious of everyone. Keeping their spirits up on the outside did not remove that inner feeling of unease as they drove out of the market car park and onto the road to Staplehurst.

Evelyn's thoughts had instinctively been for the girls, but logic seemed to sow the seed in their minds that Bob's mother was the prime candidate for such an emergency. On the road through Staplehurst they toyed with the idea of checking on Ann at her work but Bob's mother's was probably it, yes it'll be your Mum Bob. A worried mind plays tricks for which there is no accounting, willing it to be someone less loved, less needy, less important. They headed for Crit Hall where Michael informed them that Ann was dead. She had been in an accident on her motor cycle somewhere on the Sissinghurst road. She had been taken to Pembury Hospital and pronounced dead on arrival. These short stabbing sentences, punctuating the flashes of hurt and disbelief. It can't be our Ann. It must be a mistake.

Bob went to Pembury Hospital to identify her clothes and see to other formalities.

The shock was devastating. No one imagines, expects, or believes their children may pre decease them. In every day life we say 'bye' or 'cheerio' expecting them to return the way they always do. If there was ever any doubt we would never let them out of our sight; but life isn't that way and life was cruel to Bob and Evelyn that eighteenth day of May1981.

Ann had left on her motor cycle before Bob and Evelyn that morning and struck a stationary lorry on the Sissinghurst road killing her outright. Had Bob and Evelyn not needed to go to Benenden with the logs they would have come upon the accident themselves. Fate spared them this; yet in the ponderings of grief Evelyn may have even wished to have been with her daughter at that fateful moment. As it was Ann died instantly, and alone. Her grieving parents and friends wondering was it an insect? Did a rabbit run across the road? Did she skid?

Grief can be shaken off with time; it's never cured however and lives deep in the subconscious to surface on bad days. Bob and Evelyn dealt with it together 'and separately'. Already Evelyn's strength of character, more dominant since Bob's driving ban and later disablement, took charge, looking forward and living openly with the memory of their bright and talented daughter. A plan had formed within days that they would find and present a trophy named after Ann to be competed for in perpetuity.

But before Evelyn's enlightened and positive approach both had been crippled by grief. A grief few of us ever get through life without, disabling the mind from inside, making the days long and pointless. Bob was less able to cope, bottling up his feelings, until the only emotion he could release was anger, snapping uncontrollably at those he thought should have responded and turning away from those who did so.

There was no counselling in those days, no formal, or municipal sort anyway. Counselling was always an aunt or uncle for the young or a friend if you were older. It was Bob's friends George Babbage and Bill Lambert who filled the breach and finally broke through the dulling disablement that had forced him back to drink.

George and Bill picked Bob up one morning and took him down to Wittersham Road Station at Rolvenden Layne where they walked along the dykes and likely watched the Herons rise; the Snipe flying crookedly before them and felt the pushy marsh breeze on their faces. Perhaps; where they talked about old times, Good times, bad times and the mishaps and mess-ups of their own lives; where they would be indiscreet about the common things no one ever talks about, except to close friends. Gradually Bob came through, repaired by friendship and nature and time; saved after a ten days binge; the only thing he had found easily would deaden his sadness.

Since Bob had been threatened with prison he had laid off the drink. He'd taken stock and been a reformed model of the best of himself; best because his ankle and his hip niggled at his nature more frequently these days. Ann's death then was a double tragedy. As often happens, solace and common sense come from unexpected places but it has to be said that often it is the undertaker that provides reasoning to the bereaved. John Fuggle was no exception. At a time when Bob was cutting the ground from anyone who wanted to show their concern, care or respect, because he couldn't take it himself; it was John Fuggle who provided the calm reasoned explanation for the way people were.

Ann had been a lover of horses, she lived and breathed horses, it was only right that her memory could live on through a trophy. But, said Evelyn, not a trophy that could be bought by the biggest cheque book in the county won over and over again by the privileged, no, a trophy aimed at some youngster that maybe didn't even have his or her own horse. This was the decision.

A good friend Michael Hook from Rolvenden who was working in London on the stock exchange at that time volunteered to look out for a trophy and spent his lunch hours trolling through the antique shops looking for something suitable. At last his search was rewarded and they all went up to town together to look at several possibilities deciding on a beautiful forty two ounce solid silver punch bowl at an establishment by the name of Vokes at Hatton Garden. The Bowl had been made in 1912 by Claringtons of Regent Sreet and was jet black unpolished and without a plinth. British Gates of Biddenden supplied a piece of African Mohogany from which a plinth was turned and polished by Peter Wilkinson the woodwork master at Homewood School. The silver banding was fitted and inscribed by Richard Bicknell the father of one of Ann's friends.

The funeral at Charing crematorium was massively attended. Donations for the trophy were requested instead of flowers and realised £500 which paid for the full preparation of The Ann Luck Memorial Trophy, prize tickets and rosettes.

The first competition for Ann's Cup was held in Easter 1982 at the Blue Barn, Great Chart. Blue Barn stables leant their horses so each competitor had a strange horse to handle. The event included horse clothing, putting a bridle together, riding, team efforts, and so in the end the competitor with the most points was presented with the Cup and rosette.

The winner of that first competition was Jonathon Garret of Spot House farm. Woodchurch.

Normality

There is never a return to normality after bereavement because no one *can* return to it. A new normality must be created. The Luck's were tough enough to get back to the business of farming. Between 1970 and 80 their interests had swung away from the rearing of pigs and calves. That's not to say they didn't have any, but the inclination was now towards poultry. Just to test their tenacity the infamous hurricane of 87 intervened blocking all three lanes including the concrete road and killing most of their mature birds; wrecking the outhouses in its path; leaving them without services for ten days and a massive tree cutting and repairs bill. Most of us have tried to switch on the lights during a power cut out of force of habit, taking for granted these facilities are always available. Bob did the same trying to order chicken feed on a dead phone whilst Evelyn read out the number to him, he thinking he'd dialled wrong, she thinking he'd heard wrong, both collapsing in laughter when they realised what they were trying to achieve. To strike a blow for what is really normal in tough times Bob still went out with the gun, still had a bet on the major race meetings and still went down to the club for his drink.

They had had an arrangement with their friends the Morris's of Hayland farm to use their plucking machine, the sort of arrangement friends and especially small farmers around that time had, no money ever changed hands, they just lent each other their machinery and labour when it was needed. Now with the run up towards Christmas and the large increase in the number of birds they bought their own machine and by the winter of 1985 they were rearing three hundred and fifty geese and two hundred chickens for the Christmas demand. The picking [*plucking*] took three weeks starting at the beginning of December. Not withstanding their own plucking requirements they initiated a plucking service to cover pheasants in the shooting season too.

As for Julie, little is said of how she had coped with the loss of her sister. They were often mistaken for twins and like many families with more than one child the second or middle child often lived in the shadow of the elder one. This is never by design but comes about by the very nature of family. The first born gets full attention from parents who are at best learners, then along comes another and the second born gets half the attention and so on. The independence of children from large families is well documented, but this is no substitute in times of grief and Julie was no doubt lost without her sister, for her too a new normality had to be found.

Julie went on to marry Robert Wade in 1994 living first at Wittersham and then moving in 1996 to a hundred acres farm at Sandhurst raising beef cattle bought in from as far away as Somerset just like her parents did. *Shades of history repeating itself.* In the true traditions of her family she is still a fine horse woman competing when time allows on her thoroughbred bay gelding Charlie.

The Nineties

For Evelyn the nineties were difficult, her life with Bob had been a roller coaster, sometimes enjoyable sometimes bad, but with never a dull moment. All the emotions of life had come with being married to a man like Bob; hard times, good times, but always balancing one against the other. Suddenly the balance seemed upset; suddenly she felt put upon, as though her own emotions and her body were calling time.

Psychologically Evelyn was at a low ebb. She was still having dreadful nightmares over the loss of Whisky, and probably knew within herself the loss of a small dog was not the real seat of her troubles, but like a child's comforter, to her conscious mind the problem was the dog. Bob was sympathetic but he always had his own problems which made his sympathy transparent, after all what was the problem 'a dream about a dog?'

His wife was unwell and he couldn't see it, but then he was unwell too. If one is suffering then one doesn't see suffering in the same light. There was more to it than that. Bob had always put himself, and expected to be, at the centre of things. Things revolved around Bob, what was going on in the shadows around him had to be pretty dire for him to notice.

To understand Bob's life it is essential to understand his surroundings, his family, his environment, and his spouse. Evelyn had been on medication for epilepsy for most of her life and a change in this medication had brought on another attack in Nov 1988. and the withdrawal of her driving license in March 89. This now meant an enforced break of two and half years from driving for Evelyn and as Bob was banned the burden was greater on the farm business, the pony and trap being the only available means of getting around.

On Evelyn's initiative Toby the pony was purchased

twenty eight days after Swansea suspended Evelyn's licence and although he was broken he was very green. This in its self made extra work, feeding, grooming and mucking out. Trips to Tenterden took two hours out of their day using the trap, and it was at least a month before Toby was fully straightened out.

Toby's hitch rail was a drain pipe outside the Tenterden club and very soon he became a regular attraction there. Passers by would pet him and feed him until he soon came to know those who may have food with them. He would knucker [*whinny*] and paw the ground to get their attention and on one occasion one lady saw this performance, erroneously, as distress and marched into the club to demand who was in charge of the poor animal outside. Bob who hadn't liked her tone much and who wouldn't ever see an animal in distress anyway, actually put down his pint to explain.

'The missus has only been away five minutes.... Give him a bit of that cake you've got in yer shopping bag, that'll shut him up.'

He could have told her to mind her own business, he could have asked how she might like to try running a farm with no transport; he could have disarmed her with one of his smiles and stock phrases: *'If that hat ever has pups missus I'll ave one.'* But he did none of these things perhaps recognising her bravery, stepping into the Working men's club to represent a pony. Whether she fed Toby is not recorded.

In May 1991 Evelyn had to have an hysterectomy, a very psychological operation for any woman, mentally signalling the loss of womanhood, a sort of redundancy, the step towards a different phase of life. Not withstanding the discomfort, the burden of work about Millpond farm had preyed on her subconscious long before her convalescence had begun.

As to Bob, of course he would be concerned, but his predilection towards the demon drink prevailed. Evelyn had taken to hiding what little alcohol she had in various places, such things as sherry and cherry brandy, she put in with the chicken meal in an old milk churn outside thinking

Bob wouldn't find it. One day she decided to make a trifle and went out to the milk churn for some sherry only to discover Bob had found her cache and drunk the lot.

It's hard to say if this was the last straw. Like the loading of the proverbial camel it had probably happened over time. After twenty eight years of unstinting loyalty there was something about this last selfish act that was the last straw. In its self it is only what Evelyn would have predicted for she knew Bob's weaknesses better that than he did. The ensuing confrontation led to Evelyn engaging a solicitor and ultimately to marriage guidance for them both.

Throughout their marriage both had had reserves of strength complementary to the others. Evelyn was a willing follower and Bob had led through his sense of fun, his incorrigible humour and hard work. Now the teamwork failed through no fault of theirs, Bob was ill through years of hard work against the land, an unremitting adversary, this plus his habitual drinking fuelled his life long high blood pressure, but there was something more.

Over the following months however their differences were resolved. A marriage that had given them so much; through which they had struggled to make a success of life and family wasn't to be given up lightly. Evelyn's efforts, the Bar B Q's the clay shoots so popular on Bob's birthdays lightened up this flagging teamwork and soon took away some of the emotional pain.

No stranger, no close friend even, however observant would have seen Bob's suffering behind his eyes. Of course there were the physical signs the limp and the gout, he'd taken to wearing stout slippers with Velcro fastenings, even went shooting in them, but his face always spelled out fun. Even if Bob was done a disservice his response, however venomous would always contain humour, as though placed there for his antagonists to grasp and cool whatever situation there was.

But Bob *was* suffering. Like the vixen that had lost its leg and got on with the job of raising its cubs, Bob shrugged off the hurt and stoically went about the business of being Bob. He even, after years of never riding a horse mounted a big hunter in the paddock at Millpond farm to his obvious delight and to the fearful amusement of his wife.

Bob on Hunter at Millpond Farm

It took Evelyn to finally persuade, nag, or more appropriately Badger him into going to see the doctor, something he hated, having had his fill of doctors and hospitals. I'll come in with you she had said. *'You bloody won't, I'll go on my own.'* He'd replied.

They met up in the Vine Ph. some time later and of course Evelyn wanted to know what the result of his visit was. As Bob related the details he noticed there was a chap in the corner of the bar half hiding his face behind his newspaper but taking in everything Bob said. This was to trigger off Bob's sense of fun, for he winked and nodded towards the corner and immediately raised his voice to give a running commentary of what had just happened at the doctors, even though most of it was make believe.

'Course first off I ad to drop mi trousers, so's the quack could look up mi arse and see if mi cap was on crooked or not. Then he ups and takes a blood sample ter check mi for that there aids HIV thingy...then there's that coughin business for the old hernia, never warmed his ands neither...'

After a few minutes of Bob's imaginative medical recital, the gent with the paper had had enough and got up and left.

'That's stopped the farting in the church.' Bob laughed.

Of course the truth was very much different. Bob's long standing ankle, hip, high blood pressure, arthritis and ulcer had prevented him getting insurance years ago. Perhaps a knowledgeable bystander would have guessed, knowing Bob's predilection towards the drink that a liver problem might have been added to the list, but no, Bob was told on this occasion he had a lung infection and water retention.

'Water retention!' Bob might have exclaimed. *'How did that get in there?'*

August 10th 1998

August the tenth 1998 was the hottest day of that summer. Ninety one degrees Fahrenheit. Sunday, the day before, had been scorching but this morning the heat was burning the mist off the tree tops across the valley towards Potts wood and forecast was, more heat.

In and about Millpond farm the routine of running the place had changed, their diversification towards D.I.Y. livery and grazing for livestock on Evelyn's initiative kept the business viable and manageable in view of Bob's increasing inactivity. Bob's routine was the livestock, hobbling about on his sore legs watering the ducks and the geese, sorting the corn and the meal, all the husbandry that goes with farming.

It is the routine, the methodical way we run our daily lives that seduces our minds into the tranquil acceptance that it will always be thus. Punctuated by holidays, birthdays, Christmas's all, like childbirth, uniquely foreseeable. All programmed changes in our lives but nevertheless part of our routine.

Today, Monday, was a new week and Evelyn and Bob had business in Tenterden. As Bob always said a visit to the office as quality surveyor was a must, the office being the Vine Ph.. But also the calendar had for Bob a programmed booze cruise on the Tuesday, so he'd need some cash for that trip too.

They were home again by twelve and by now the heat was bouncing back off the concrete; the birds were standing on one leg feathers fanned out or luxuriating in the dust hollows under the hedgerows. Even the mallard on the pond at Penhill were quietly subdued somewhere in the deep shade of the surrounding willows.

Bob and Evelyn made for the house, only marginally cooler. Bob sat in his regular spot close to the window and spread out the Daily Mail they'd picked up from the pipe at the end of the concrete road.

Soon they were enjoying lunch; salad days always brings out the cheese and tomatoes to go with the crusty bread and now, stilted conversation on how nice if it would rain or predictions of thunder later.

Evelyn took yesterday's Mail out into the garden and found shade under the trees. Bob had struggled to keep his eyes open, Evelyn had noticed that, even she could have napped; there wasn't a breath of air, not a zephyr to move the leaves anywhere.

In the house, even the manageable concept of the tabloid, a boon for a generation of readers with arm ache; saw that Bob's copy was best spread out across the table, the near corners held down by his elbows and his head resting on his hands. That way he'd only need to lift and eyebrow to keep a look out for that 'Jay!'

For all Bob's ailments, never was there any suspicion he may have had a heart problem. Of course Evelyn knew he was unwell and her observations had forced him to take medical advice, even e.c.g.'s, at the hospital he dreaded so much; and he'd been cleared. After all, the high blood pressure he'd had all his life, the diagnosed ulcer, the touch of jaundice were all part of Bob's current existence.

It would be shortly after two o clock when the terriers howled and Evelyn got up thinking it signalled a fox nearby; a reflex of a lifetime for a poultry keeper, for no self respecting fox would be abroad in this heat. She went down to the house....

Bob's death was of course an immense shock to Evelyn. Bob had passed away as he read, the sounds of the garden birds in his ears, his terriers at his feet like an ancient warrior and just perhaps that old Jay bird canting its head on the fence post outside the window.

Epilogue

Bob's funeral and service took place the following Monday the 17th August. [his birthday]. The service at St Mildred's church Tenterden was attended by family, friends and admirers, fellows of the clubs and pubs across the county, from the farming and shooting fraternity, the markets and the Ashford Valley hunt, the Tally-ho club and the town of Tenterden.

His Eulogy was read by his good friend Gordon Lilly and was so tinged with the humour of Bob's life you might swear he had been at the writer's elbow. Yet, no eulogy, no biography can ever collect together the real qualities of this mischievous countryman. Bob was no academic, no scientist, no war hero, nothing like that, but he was the spice that makes a country region what it is. He was linked to nature in a way that few of us are, close to the soil of his beloved Kent. They say man is immortal through his sons, his progeny; here we have a man immortal through the memory of him, his stories his pranks and adventures, his attitude to life and the lives of his fellows.

For those who know the little lake surrounded by trees near Millpond farm where Kingfishers can be watched in the summer, where Mallard live the year round; It is this little haven from the hottest days with its cool lush grass banks where Bob would see the Swallows dipping at flies and hear the Hornets buzz, this is where Bob Luck now lies in his own preciously hallowed ground.

Acknowledgements

Evelyn Luck gratefully acknowledges being able to use the following images in this publication.

Image 1: Photo Mick Crook.
Image 2: Photo Mick Crook.
Image 3: Photo. Douglas Weaver.
Image 7: The Kent Messenger.
Image 8: The Kentish Express.
Image 9. Photo Mick Crook
Image 10. Photo George Babbage
Image 12: The Kent & Sussex Courier.
Image 18: Photo Mick Crook.
Rear cover plate. Rob Tompsett RTPhoto's

And extends her thanks to
Alan and Sheila Palmer of Smarden, For access to their Archival and historic aviation details of Headcorn Air field.
And to
Caye Gould of The Ashford Writers Group, for research help.
And to
The many friends and acquaintances of both old and young Bob Luck for their contributions large and small.

Printed in the United Kingdom
by Lightning Source UK Ltd.
9740300001B/91-162

9 781843 750543